American

MW01230331

Diaspora Road in Ghana

Kali Sichen

LIBRARY OF CONGRESS

LCCN: 2023901905

Copyright: 2006-2023 by Kali Sichen; ©2023

North Scale Institute Publishing; Atlanta, Georgia Territory [30349]

Printed in the United States at North America; Amaruca, Al Moroc, Aztlan; Turtle Island

Cover: Painting by John Floyd, Jr. Atlanta; Georgia Territory. Depicting Warrior Queen Califia at Pacific Ocean, prepared to meet friend or foe, with Mt. Shasta in the background.

Graphics: Nana-Esi Igyan; Formatting: Sofi Igyan

ISBN: 978-0-916299-09-5

Acknowledgments

This part of my journey to complete this book, the stories that were written from 2006 through 2010, is accomplished now only because I have grown into my Soul's New Birth in this realm.

In 2011, I asked *Sankofa,* a trusted friend, to make corrections in grammar and other editing suggestions. *Sankofa,* an artist and a sensitive Soul, was very pleased to do this. I am forever indebted to her for her kindness and keen eye. She suggested, however, that I should not go forward to publish this work at that time. I was not pleased; but I heeded her suggestion, nevertheless.

The world was on the brink of a major transformation. Truth emerged from centuries of lies and deceptions. Now, 12 years after this journey began, I am transformed, the entire world is transformed.

I also want to thank my immediate family, my grandchildren especially, because they continue to guide me through these technical aspects of publishing this work. A special shout-out goes to three of my informative YouTube Historians; Dane Callaway (I'm Just Here to Make You Think); Kurimeo Ahau (Rise of the Amaru Khans); Uriah Brandon (UB.TV); and Taj Tarik Bey (House of Reawakening Minds); and Chief Pontiac. They have played a major role in directing me toward historical publications that reveal the TRUTH about America, our home, our heritage.

TABLE OF CONTENTS

Introduction

What is it about a land that is so special, so desired, the entire history of that land and the entire history of the original people of that land had to be covered up, flooded over, torn down, hidden, decimated, and completely re-write their history. What is it about that land and the original people of that land that was so desired by the rest of the world's inhabitants that a worldwide conspiracy of silence would inundate that land? The many races of the world would then merge together to overtake the original people, use them, abuse the people, villainize the people and attempt to de-humanize the original people in an attempt to assume their identity? What could it be about this group of people, about their land, that would cause the world to conspire to secretly agree to remove them, to *"snuff them out"*, to pretend that they don't exist?

Legends throughout the world tell of brothers who competed, usually one who was jealous of the other and who either killed his brother or who usurped the brother's identity and/or his inheritance. How is it that *"holy books"* throughout the world's cultures tell the same or similar stories about the *"warring brothers"*? Why is it that, in the closing days of the Age of Pisces, the 2160-year cycle of stars, that this "Age of Deception" would culminate in the exposure of the criminal conspiracy against these people and their land? Most importantly, why is it that so many of these people are so *"lost"* that they can't see the "conspiracy" perpetrated against them?

The purpose of this book is not to answer these questions. There are volumes written already, both Truths – to wake these very special people up, and Lies – to keep them asleep, and ignorant to their own inheritance. I speak about the Original, Organic, Indigenous Americans, those who were referred to as "*Indians*" when Europeans "*colonizers*" landed on these shores with the written "intent" from the head of the Church of Rome, was to take over the land and destroy the people. The Original people were called the "copper-colored" races who were living peacefully when the European arrived in 1492. This is according to the history that the world has been taught. Since colonization their identity has changed from Indian to Mulatto, Negro, Afro, Afro-American, African American to Black. In other words, being "black" means that they don't exist. They are NOT a part of the human family because they have no lineage. They are not recognized in the Law of any land. With this "Black tag" they have no line of descent.

This is one of the greatest deceptions of the Piscean Age, for these are the only people who, according to Western science, are 100% human. All other races have traces of DNA from sub-humanoids of this planet, i.e., Neanderthals. This is not my belief, it is the "*science*" that we have been taught is the supreme knowledge on this, our Mother Earth. The only "**TRUE HUMANS**" on this planet, GAIA, are the "**BLACK**" people, the ORIGINAL PEOPLE, the ORGANIC PEOPLE, the original Indians and Africans.

When the planet Pluto entered Capricorn in 2008, the zodiac sign that rules over governments and institutions of authority and ruler-ship, I was deep into my own inner transformation and life changing events. I had distanced myself from family, putting 11,000 nautical miles between my home and my business partner (husband) of 30 years. I was on a vision quest, to examine my inner life, my beliefs, and the core of my reasons for incarnating in this life at this time, in this era of global change. I was searching for my true *"Mission"*, my *"Unction"*.

Even though my life was full, exciting, and eventful, my heart was heavy. Early in life, in my early twenties, I was on a mission, a spiritual quest. Yes, even though I was very young, I knew that I had a greater role to play other than being a wife, a mother, a grandmother, and a worker. I envisioned myself sitting on the side of a tall mountain, meditating, in deep thought and seeking solutions to the many challenges facing humanity. Pluto heralds in long-term changes, especially powers of authority and ruler-ship, power, money, governments, religious and educational institutions, those established foundations that define a society. These institutions define an era, dictate the power structure, and determine who rules. At the founding of America, Pluto was in the sign of Capricorn. This brought what was supposed to be a **"New Age"** of Justice as *"All men are created equal"*, according to the Declaration of Independence. However, what lingered in the minds and hearts of the so called *"Founding Father's"* was the legacy of the Doctrine of Discovery. This was the leftovers from the Papal Bull of 1492 the *"Inter Caetera"* that encouraged Europeans to invade non-Christian lands, to rob, rape, kill and subdue innocent peoples and take their wealth, all in the name of converting them to Christianity.

The document, the 1776 Declaration of Independence, that most Americans believe we are living under was subverted in 1871, when a new form of government, a corporation, replaced the Republic, and the corporation of the United States, Inc. was written called into law. We were all deceived into thinking that the government was being *"Reconstructed"* for the benefit of the *"Negros"*. This was the greatest deception since the Doctrine of

Discovery. The illusion of transforming *"pagans"* into Christians, was simply outright genocide and theft of land and resources. The same is true about the era of **"Reconstruction"** after the so called **"Civil War"** in America. In 1871 the Aboriginal, Indigenous peoples of the land called America, were the so called *"Negros"*. The intent of the *"Reconstruction"* was to completely change the history of these so-called American states. Reconstruction removed the Identity of the Organic People, the so-called American Indians, and named them *"Negros"*. Over the years, the *"Negros'* land was taken away from them, through theft, subversion, color of law and intimidation. Any Negro who called himself an *"Indian"* was hanged as a sport after church on Sundays. This was the entertainment of the European peasants who were awarded the stolen lands of the true Americans, the *"copper-colored Tribes"* of the America's.

For this reason, and because of the *"compulsory education"*, the indoctrination centers called *"schools"*, most American Indians have forgotten their true Identity. It wasn't until the 1940's that the idea was created and promoted that the **"Negro"** had been brought to America on *"slave ships"*. The indoctrination centers, the Hollywood movie industry, the **Tel-Lie'vision** and the Madison Avenue Mind Control Advertising Industry went to work to change the Image of the American Indians. Wave after wave of new immigrants were brought to these shores to replace the Organic, Indigenous Americans. They were supported by the United States Corporation, given jobs, business loans, land, houses, education, and rights that were denied to the Original Americans. These *"new immigrants"* were taught to look down on the Organic Americans, to ridicule them and disrespect them. They even get away with *"murdering"* the

8

Original Americans who are "***Lost at Home***".

It's hard to find TRUTH in Apartheid America. The indoctrination is so pervasive, so deep. The most highly educated are often the hardest to reach! It is for this reason that the title of this book is "**American Indians Searching for Home**".

All the stories are true. They were written from my own personal experiences between 2006 and 2010 during the time of my residence in a small coastal village in Ghana, West Africa. The names of people and places are either omitted or changed, so that I would not offend anyone. My attempt is only to share my thoughts and my feelings, my growth, and my challenges as, through study and knowledge of REAL history, I moved from African American to Indigenous American. All Praises to the *Great Spirit, the Great One on High, the Great Mother of the Universe.*

Corrections and Historical Truths

AMERICAN INDIANS SEARCHING FOR HOME

So, you ask, how is it that an American Indian is seeking a "**Home**" outside of their native land of America? What has been kept as the biggest secret of American history is *"what is the identity of the true American Indians"*. This is the elephant in the room in every lesson, every history book, every classrooms in America. How is this?

First, let us clarify the names. I used the name "Indian" because this is the name that most people understand the "Indigenous Americans" to be. But this is only the first misconception. When I was a child in America's school system, history taught us from grade school:

Fourteen hundred ninety-two Columbus sailed the ocean blue. He had three ships and left from Spain; He sailed through sunshine, wind and rain.
He sailed by night; he sailed by day; He used the stars to guide his way.
Ninety sailors were on board; Some men sailed while others snored.
Then the workers went to sleep; And others sailed the ocean deep.
Day by day they looked for land; They dreamed of trees and rocks and sand.
October 12 their dreams came true; You never saw a happier crew!
Then in fourteen hundred ninety-two, Columbus sailed the ocean blue.

Every Child in America learned this rhyme. It was the first step in the indoctrination of the false narrative called *"American History"*.

The next indoctrination came when the story was told that Columbus was looking for another "route" to India. Now where was this "India"? The truth is that, in his personal diary, Columbus knew that he was traveling to a place that he called the "Holy Land". (***The Diario of Christopher Columbus' First Voyage – 1492-1493: Abstracted by Fray Bartolomé de las Casas***). The country that we know of as "India" today was known at Columbus' time as "Hindustan." It was incorporated and named India in 1947.

This false narrative is what gave the Aboriginal, Indigenous people, the people who were already occupying this *"Holy Land"*, the name Indians. In this first edition of biographical notes that I am presenting in this publication, I am correcting terminology that has kept the TRUTH about American history and the Aboriginal people the quiet "elephant of disinformation" in the room of indoctrinated *"facts"*.

The next historical *"disinformation facts"* of American history is that Columbus was looking for the "New World". Now, how could they believe this to be the New World when they were told that their own historians, like Plato, who spoke about the existence of a land beyond the great *"Ethiopian Sea"* (Atlantic Ocean) known as *"Atlantis"*, that was the home of a highly advanced civilization? At that time, any learned European knew

11

that there existed a land beyond the borders of Eurasia and Ethiopia (Africa), a land of gold and silver, pearls and abundant food and exotic animals and riches beyond the scope of anything that was known in Europe at that time. Seafarers, merchants and traders such as the **Phoenicians or Moors,** had for many years traded with these civilizations of *"Atlantis"*, which they had quietly kept secret from most of the European countries. During this time, around the 15th century, during the expulsion of the **Moors and Sephardic Jews** from Spain, America was known as the *"land of milk and honey"* and was desirous by European.

Who were the Aboriginal people who were encountered by the first explorers? They were certainly NOT the "savages" that were taught about in the indoctrination centers that were "compulsory education centers" known as "schools". There is a map published by the National Geographic Society published in 2007. This map, **A WORLD TRANSFORMED**, depicts the Eastern coasts of the present United States from 1491 to 1800. It shows the Aboriginal Cultures as "thriving" before the arrival of the Europeans. The coastal communities lived in well-built houses called "long houses", not in tents. Their villages were well organized, fortified and mostly enclosed by tall timbers. There were cultivated fields and canals for bringing water into the villages. There were clear rivers and lakes with abundant fish that were often caught by hand, by hand-held nets and woven baskets. Abundant food was cultivated, with corn, beans, squash, pumpkins and gourds being the major crops. There was also cultivated tobacco, which was a ceremonial crop.

Douglas Ubelaker, Professor of Anthropology at Colombian School of the Arts, was one of the major contributors to the statistics on this map. He based his "facts" on the scanty information from European explorers whose documents he had.

POPULATIONS IN AMERICA

	1500	1650	1800
INDIANS	1,002,000	379,000	178,000
EUROPEANS		58,000	4,763,000
AFRICANS		1,600	1,002,000

This is the information touted as "**facts**" by the **NATIONAL GEOGRAPHIC** and the **SMITHSONIAN INSTITUTE**. Within 150 years we are told that the Europeans brought over almost 6 times more "Africans" than there were surviving "*Indians*" and that they, the Europeans, outnumbered the "*Indians,*" and "*Africans*" combined by 6 to 1. This must be the biggest "*fairy tale*" since "*Columbus discovered America*"!

I suggest that all who think that this may be a legitimate "*fact*", please check resources other than the easily accessible **WIKIPEDIA** and institutional "*historians*" from American Universities and "**Think Tanks**" for validation.

So, who are the "*Africans*" who were brought over in sailboats by Europeans? These sailboats, powered by the wind only, had to make at least 6,680 voyages within 150 years. Each boat had to carry the crew, and the passengers with a cargo of rum, firearms, and consumer goods for the Europeans. There were no sailboats capable of this manner of cargo AND people on the 4–6-week journey. The first powered "steamboat" crossed the Atlantic in 1819, twenty years after these above

13

given statistics. Do your own research and see what actual *"facts"* you can find outside of the institutional, *"academic narrative."*

One source that is considered to be most authentic in its description of America before the onslaught of the **non-melanated** Europeans, is the book by James Adair, Esquire, a Trader with the Indians, and Resident in their Country for Forty years, first published in 1775: ***"The History of the American Indians."*** In this extensive account of, not only what he personally observed, but what he experienced by living among the people for more than four generations. He described the tribes mostly of the Southeastern woodlands, from the Mississippi River to the eastern shores, from the Gulf of Mexico north toward Maryland and Tennessee. They were of a ***"copper-color"*** from a light color copper to a very dark copper or reddish-brown. *He described their dietary, ceremonial, and religious practices, and was convinced that they were* **descendants of the Hebrews**, in fact, the **Lost Tribes of Israel**.

He observed that the spoken languages there were many words that were exactly the same as ancient Hebrew. He put forth arguments, as would an Attorney (Esquire), for his case, presenting twenty-three (23) arguments, detailing how he came to the conclusions he documented about the original people of America. His case studies were specifically about the Katahba Nation, the Cheerake Nation, the Muskohge Nation the Choktah Nation and the Chikkasah Nation. These are the exact way that he spelled their names.

In 1924 a Virginia government employee and eugenicist, Walter Plecker, in the Vital Statistics office, created the "**Racial Integrity Act**". The sole purpose of this *"Act"* was to re-classify

14

the Organic Peoples of Virginia. Every person was classified as either *"white"* or *"colored"*. Racial mixing was prohibited and the classification of *"Indian"* was removed from the records. From that point forward, all Aboriginal, Indigenous Virginians officially lost their identity. Many States followed Virginia's lead robbed and wrote the Indigenous people out of their true status in *"law."*

Now, we still don't know who the *"Africans"* were! There was no historical information about twelve million *"Africans"* being transported to the North American colonies before the stories became a part of the *"history books"* in the compulsory education system during the 1940's. The *"Negros"* who were first called African descendants came from the creation by Melville Herskovits, a Jewish American of immigrant parents and anthropologist who wrote a book entitled **"The Myth of the Negro Past"**. This was one of the first links made by an American (immigrant) anthropologist writer or scholar between Africans and American **"Negros"**. It was at this time that these *"anthropologists"* began to write about and coin the "A**frican American**" theory. They were helped along by none other than W. E. B. Dubois, descendant of French and Dutch Huguenot immigrants, who is also touted as one of the progenitors of the *"Out of Africa"* theory created by German Jewish Franz Boas and Melville Herskovits, both recent immigrants. It took 550 years for the *"theory"* of the African origin of Negros (*Indians*) in America to develop.

So, who are the Negros that the "**theory"** of African origins is supposedly about? Well, what if we say that these "Negros" had a "status" and "name change" from 1492 until 1950 at least six

15

times. First, they were called Indians, then they were called *Mulattoes*, then they were *Colored*, back to *Negro*, then they were called *Moors*, then *Afro-Americans*, then *African Americans* and now *Blacks*. Why was the name change so necessary for the same group of people? Is it because they were and are the **TRUE** inhabitants, the **REAL** Americans, the Aboriginal, Indigenous **owners of this the** *"Holy Land"*? **Yes! Finally, we get to the TRUTH.**

All this dialog, giving historical TRUTHS, exposing the *"facts"* of this *"compulsory education system"* called schools, starting in kindergarten through PHD (Doctor of Philosophy) programs (pogroms?) are truly *"disinformation dissemination institutions"* whose main objective was to ROB the ORIGINAL, ORGANIC, AMERICANS of their, LAND, IDENTITY, MINERAL WEALTH, LANGUAGES and their CULTURE. It may be difficult for many Americans to accept these TRUTHS, because the indoctrination is so perverse and so deep, most Americans, even those *"disenfranchised Americans"* will reject these TRUTHS.

One thing that I must add, a TRUTH that is mostly unknown to Americans, that despite all the horrors of the *"pogroms"* put upon the Aboriginal, Indigenous, Organic Peoples of the Americas, both North and South America, they have remained the most creative, most ingenious, most culturally innovative people of the entire world. The whole world follows the movements of American Aboriginals in music, dance, clothing, hair styles, and most surprising to the entire world, engineering and technological innovation. Yes, we have been ROBBED of even our technological and engineering inventions, that were wrongly given and accredited to the foreign oppressors, mostly from Europe, Asia the Middle East, and North Africa.

16

All the above information was necessary for the reader to know why the title of this book: **"American Indians Searching for Home,"** is necessary. Perhaps now, you can understand that even they, the so called *"American Indians,"* may think that their home is someplace else.

Castelo de São Jorge da Mina

Elmina Castle (*Dungeon)* was built by the Portuguese in 1482. It is the first trading post built by Portuguese on the Gulf of Guinea and the oldest structure built by European (**Moors & Sephardic Jews merchants & traders**) south of the Sahara.

PROLOGUE
The Road between Two Castles
Passageways through the Dungeons

To many they are called castles; to others they are decried as dungeons. It really depends on which side of the gate you are standing – and who's holding the key.

At the age of sixty-one I ran away from home. I knew that I could not continue to live under the circumstances. My mistake through the years was to suffer in silence. The world thought that everything was fine – just hunky-dory. Even when I left home very few people knew the circumstances; many still don't. But at this point it really doesn't matter.

I was destined to climb to the ramparts and steeples of castles and ramble through the pits of their dungeons where the cries of my captured and chained ancestors still echoed in the chambers. There were chains on my mind as well; I had to be cleansed, purified and sanctified before I was released.

It was certainly no accident that a seaside cottage became available to me just a few days after I reached Elmina. From the plateau just above the crashing waves of the Great Mame Wata sometime called the Atlantic Ocean, and in view of the castle and dungeons of Cape Coast on my left and Elmina castle and dungeons on my right, I gazed for hours into blackness of the moonless nights. I danced to the music of Stevie Wonder when the silvery glitter of the full moon turned the ocean waves into giant puffs of foamy whip cream. I slept. I rested. My heart found a small space to lie down for a little while. It was a true blessing.

19

There was much work for me to do with myself. Liberating my soul from a self-imposed bondage was far more difficult than I thought it would be. I had chained myself to a love-less relationship. I had to find my brave heart once again. In the years of service to the relationship I forgot who I was. It was good for him but devastating to me. My journey to self-realization unfolds in the following pages.

On the road between two castles aka Diaspora Road

God Lives in Africa

Catchy phrases and popular sayings have a way of being uttered without any real consideration for their meaning. Like when, after visiting Africa, the popular motion picture and television superstar, Will Smith declared to his adoring American audience that "God lives in Africa", I wasn't quite sure what he meant, and if he saw the same sights, sounds, smells, tastes, smiles, tears, laughter and reverences that I experience when I am in various African nations.

I'm certain Will Smith has not seen some of the back streets in shanty towns and remote villages of Africa that I have seen. No doubt, his hosts and sponsors on his African nation tours have kept him away from some of the more unsightly and horrific scenes that one finds in any poverty-ridden place of earth, including America.

I see very ordinary life events as I walk the back road of these small villages on the Atlantic coast. Because access to the internet is a challenge, early mornings I stroll to the nearest resort hotel to use their business center four or five times a week. Sometimes I travel the main road, and if the sun is too hot, I can easily take a shared taxi ride from the hotel junction to the muddy road to my beach front house. More often, I walk the back street, through tiny villages, where, early mornings, I see children bathing, soaping themselves completely before pouring a small pan of water over their shiny bodies, or adults brushing their teeth vigorously with a small cup of water in hand. There are the sheep trekking through the grasses, tasting tidbits of luscious morsels of grass. There are pigmy goats climbing the rocks, testing their mountain climbing agility in search of more interesting patches of grass and wild flowers of the deep coastal gullies, while at the same time defying the waves at the ocean front.

This village road was paved at one time, during the days of President Osagyefo Dr. Kwame Nkrumah, when this village passage road was the only access to the Elmina Beach Chalets. Before the resort hotel was built, these tiny chalets were the weekend retreat for the rulers, the ministers and members of parliament of this new African nation. Those tiny chalets were thrown to the wayside, to make room for the sprawling beach resort hotel. The road through the village was replaced by a major two lane highway, and the village passage fell into total disrepair. Here and there lay patches of pavement that are reminiscent of the days of glory when Ghana was riding high, head to the sky, shoulders back and chest out, with full knowledge that God had a new agenda for Africa, and Ghana was leading the way.

During this rainy season, this back road posed a great problem, with the puddles of muddy water that had to be navigated to continue the journey to the hotel. One particular puddle was a real ordeal; it was almost the size of a small pond. Tall grass grew on both sides, and the sides of the puddle were like a slippery creek-bed, showing signs of other passers by who have already slipped into the muddy ravine. On several occasions, I almost turned around to seek the main road, but decided that I would meet the obstacle instead. I would hold tight to the tall grass, praying that it would hold and not break to leave me tumbling into the muddy waters.

23

I will never forget the day when I saw an older woman standing in the middle of that same mud puddle, taking the water in hand and putting it to her mouth. She would slush the water around and spit it out. The last handful I saw her swallow, and I said, *"God lives in Africa"*. Here is a puddle of water that has been standing for at least 6 weeks, people and cars trekking through it, goats and sheep marching through, and this old woman is drinking from it!

I was so dumb-founded that I thought that I would be speechless as I approached the elder. I managed to smile and greet her, "Good Morning"; she smiled and replied, "Good Morning, Madame." I walked away, thinking that only an African could drink that water and survive, because God walks with them!

Several weeks later, as the rains were beginning to subside, and the puddle was getting smaller, from a distance I eyed an old man who was bent over in the same muddy puddle. As I approached, I saw him removing what looked to me like rags, but which could possibly have been his only clothing. He pulled them from a shaggy rice sack, one by one, and dipped them into the puddle. At a closer view, it appeared that he was doing his laundry. As I approached and passed him, with warm greetings and exchange of smiles, I uttered to myself, *"God lives in Africa."*

Weeks after, I was sitting with a village elder on my comfortable screened veranda, overlooking the waves splashing against the rocks. He began to give me some history of this small village. Before the return of the people from the Aboriginal Diaspora, who somehow have inhabited the far end of this once famous road to Nkrumah's beach chalets, the village people never crossed the road to this beach-front side. It was sacred grounds, where the ancestors dwelled and one had to be prepared to meet them with alms and gifts and reverence, when you visited this side of the road, near the beach.

Interestingly, this same road leading to Nkrumah's beach chalets continues on through the historical, ancient town of Elmina, where it meanders through the village center and finally leads to the bridge across the *River Benya* onto the infamous Castle at Elmina. It is possible that this same road was used to drive the captured Africans to their final destination, the "**Door of No Return**", the Dungeons of Elmina where many Africans were carted onto ships, headed for the auction blocks, mostly to Brazil in South America.

The lore and legend of the people whose ancestors watched as their mothers and fathers, brothers and sisters, aunties and uncles, cousins and friends, marched past their huts, never to be seen again, remain with them, an ancestral memory of fear for their own survival. That other side of road held the mournful cries of their people who, after disappearing into the holds of the castle, vanished from their homes forever!

Often, things are not what they appear to be. It is with knowledge that you know the true meaning and the true value of a puddle of muddy water. That muddy puddle may not have been what I thought it was at all. It could have been where the ancestors took their bath, and the spirits dwelled within bestowing their blessing and protection.

We, who think that we are educated, sophisticated and knowledgeable, often miss the true meanings of simple things, because their meaning is not on the surface, they are occult, hidden from view, and accessible only to those who open their hearts to truth. I am humbled, knowing that those of us who have come to dwell on this beach side of the road, which you could very well call it **Diaspora Road** are sitting with those ancestors who have remained here, waiting for their return. I pray that in our ignorance of their ways and their truths, that we do not make stupid mistakes and copy the behavior of those wicked Europeans who captured and took them away from these shores. I pray for the ancestral guidance and their blessings.

Epilogue

My daughter and I took the children for an outing at a beach resort toward the western end and just off the Diaspora Road. The resort is past the *infamous slave dungeon* known as Elmina Castle. Posted on the resort bulletin board were photos of famous visitors, and Will Smith, the actor who said that *"God lives in Africa"*, was among them. I realized then that, indeed, Will Smith had witnessed the teaming life, the music and rhythm of the people who continue to thrive in the shadow of one of the most wretched chapters in the history of mankind, the **Trans-Atlantic Slave Trade**. Yes, Will Smith's eyes did witness the miracle of the survival of the African people who, in spite of all the odds, continue to thrive living so close to the earth, so close to God. *God truly lives in Africa.*

For the people to still be kicking strong after the hundreds of years that that have passed since the strongest and most able bodies were stolen away and sold into slavery on foreign soil is a testimonial to God's protection of their race. Under similar circumstances and during the same time frame other races have fallen almost into extinction. Ironically, those wretched soles responsible for the dastardly deed of slavery are themselves falling into extinction. *Truly, God lives in Africa,* and God will continue to breathe the sacred breath of life into **Her Original People.**

My Life is a Meditation
The Sun's Ingress into Taurus

It was a very thoughtful and compassionate email from someone whom I never met, who is a friend of my dear friend. A friend from my youthful days in San Francisco shares my writings with many of her friends in Mid-Western USA. I appreciate the sharing, because I feel that my commentaries on life in Ghana in 2006-07 can be a useful yardstick for my fellow Diaspora Africans who are considering visiting the Motherland, retiring to the Motherland or one who is looking for an excuse not to do either. These commentaries are especially important to my age group, the Baby Boomers, who are now fast approaching retirement, and after years of service to family, community and the *"land where our fathers slaved"*; they are looking for a little comfort, pampering and leisure in their mature years as elders. Ghana is to be considered as a retreat for retirement!

This wonderful email suggested that I go *"inside myself"* to find peace; that I should *"light a candle and meditate"*, and suggested that I should "pray and ask for guidance". All of these are wonderful suggestions; surely, they come from someone who does not know me. This last year of my life has been a constant prayer, a prolonged meditation, and a deep voyage within. In other words, this year has been a voyage to the center of myself. It has been an exercise in patience, learning a greater compassion, implementing a deep understanding, and casting aside per-conceived ideas and judgments based on western values and beliefs. The excavation is still in progress.

28

Back in the days of my youth in San Francisco, I longed for a mountaintop where I could escape to meditate and find inner peace and harmony within myself and in my daily affairs. I studied the world religions with intensity, seeking to find some answers to the puzzles of my daily reality. As I held a newborn babe in arms, I tackled the metaphysical, spiritual books, astronomy and the science of the stars. I longed for the days when I could devote my life to the service of humanity, after I found those spiritual answers that were straight forward enough be shared with all. I dreamed of living on the highest peak in Tibet. I gave that up because Tibet is a cold country. I decided on Mt Kilimanjaro in Kenya. It better suited my spiritual understanding of my origins, and my ancestral heritage. Now I understand why I was always seeking a mountaintop.

In Ghana each day, I awaken before daybreak with a prayer, while I listen to the sounds from the village. In the far distance, I hear a Muslim cleric calling believers to devotion; the cock next door shouts out his morning cry. There is a bustling of taxis on the highway, while early morning risers in the village start the long trek to a neighboring village to fetch water. The tiny birds whose nest is balanced on the eaves of my roof at my bedside window begin their sweet song.

I open the doors and windows to my front veranda, and smell the ocean, and out of the corner of my eye, there appears a small canoe, filled with local fishermen, who, after a busy night at sea, are hauling in their catch. They are so close to my door that I could call them, and they would hear me. I quickly dress in my walking shoes, to hit the street before the sun ascends to more than 15° above the horizon; at that point the rays are so strong that

29

they begin to burn my face.

Although I am walking at the oceanfront, I cannot access the beach because the coast is cluttered with rugged and dangerous out-cropping rocks. I walk along the Diaspora Road, and as I stroll by, I inhale the sweet fragrance of the trees lining the outer gate of the first Resort compound. The Hebrew Israelite rabbi has set a table at the next Resort on down this road. I approach an abandoned motel, with a huge grounds and beach front. It calls to me, as the white egrets, with their yellow comb, peck through the tall grasses by the entrance gate.

I walk the road through the many tiny villages that hug the coast. I admire the latest display of wildflowers embracing the dirt road, so colorful, so delicate and so beautiful. The Great Mother has taken a long brush to stroke Her most subtle colors, and painted road signs for my pleasure. The goats are climbing along the ledges of the many unfinished houses; I surmise that this is their exercise in village cliff climbing, since the rocks at the seashore pose too great a risk. The hens are pecking and scratching, while the mother leads her baby chicks on a field trip, in search of any good thing to eat. The dogs are lying around in front of the houses, in expectation of any crumbs that may be thrown their way after breakfast. The women and girls are sweeping their dirt yards clean and neat, and free of debris. I greet them all as I swiftly walk past; some of them smile, I know, because they can't understand why I would walk so fast in the mornings, carrying no load, and apparently with no particular destination.

As I round the corner at the junction where my Jamaican friends have built a beautiful guest lodge, I smell something wonderful. I look around to see a huge bush in a vacant lot, planted by the Great Mother, filled with lilac flowers that smell like the incense of paradise. Across the road there is a row of shrubs, with perfumed yellow flowers that hide another vacant lot.

As I approach the main highway on the trail back home, I encounter many things that sadden me. One long truck labors along, carrying a giant tree, so big and long, it is cut into three pieces. Only one tree can be placed on an 18-wheeler long bed truck. Even though I cry at the loss of those monuments to Mother Earth, I rejoice that I am seeing many of those giant trees return to the coastal landscape. There is much bustling as students wait for buses and parents hail taxis to take them to their day's chores. The dark soot and fumes from the unregulated truck exhaust burn my eyes and nostrils, but the trees along the road change the fragrance swiftly after the passing of the nuisance vehicles.

I return home to continue the exercise and meditation. First, my thirst is quenched with the fresh water of the coconut, just plucked from the tree. Electrolytes rush through my blood, pumping new oxygen into my muscles. I roll out my yoga mat and ball. The best cure that I have found for back ache is the yoga ball. When you reach my age, the ball helps to balance the aging body. As I carefully move into the "bow" posture, bending backwards over the big ball to reach my hands to the floor, I remain in this position for a short time. Yoga is the reason why I can still walk with a quick gait.

I am sweaty now and need to cool off. I take a cup of hot tea and sit on the veranda. My fishermen are still on the ocean within calling distance at my veranda door; their vivid, multi-colored boat is pulling, hauling, and thrusting. Today's catch must be bountiful! Hurry, I say, so that you can get to the farm before the sun begins to beat down! My prayer at the ocean side is not yet finished. I close my eyes and see the bright orange sun through my eyelids. Amen.

Dressed in loose cotton pants and a T shirt, I rush to the car and take off for the country. The journey rambles through the coastal mountains, lush with green, rolling hills. In the early mornings these mountains are hidden in a delicate mist. I turn left to head north on a dusty road, and I immediately hear the sound of that wonderful bird. I must find out her name, and see how she looks, because her voice is so sweet, and her tune so unique. I always look forward to coming to her concert at the *Moringa* farm. The wildflowers grace the road on each side, sky blue, sunlight yellow, rich gold, creamy white and the dashing red from the Flamboyant trees, *Delonix regia*. The dominant color is green, even during the dry season!

I find my way to the farm on foot; it is about ¼ kilometer from the road, through a narrow, winding path that meanders through a coconut grove. I pass a wild pineapple, juicy, red in color, and growing in a thicket among the coconut trees. The *Pra-Baah River* is filling up again, even after a few rains. I am always amazed when I emerge from the coconut grove, to find the field of light green trees, with silky, shimmering leaves, swaying in the soft morning breeze. The farm is beginning to smell like Moringa now that the plant dominates the vegetation in this valley.

I greet the farmers, who are busily playing at work,

laughing, joking enjoying their casual chores. I stroll towards the shelter, past the water well. There, I can hide from the sun. I sit a few minutes to compose myself, and my beautiful bird begins her violin concerto, a magnificent serenade. If only I could find the words to describe her song. It will come, on the right day, at the right hour. Sometimes I don't want to disturb the concert, so I stay inside the woven palm leaf shelter for a long time. The breeze flows through the woven stripes of palm fronds. I relax on my bamboo bed. When I want to see what the farmers are doing, I simply look through the cracks between the palm fronds; no one knows that I am looking.

Always there are discussions about the trees, the sowing, the weeding, the watering, the workers and, far too often, the work that is not being done. This, too, is a meditation, an intense prayer, and I hope that the *Almighty One* will walk with me, so that I can be firm and just, and do the right thing for everyone involved.

I admire the *Moringa* trees; the leaves are dainty, exquisite. The trees are growing so fast now that we are emerging from the dry season. There have been several rains, but not nearly enough. My prayer is also for rain, so that the well will fill with water, the trees will grow, and there will be many healing leaves of Moringa for the people, for the locals and our brothers, sisters and children in the Diaspora.

Returning to my ocean side cottage, it is mid-afternoon. I find the room to be somewhat cool because the curtains were drawn, and room darkened to keep out the heat of the sunlight. I open the door to the veranda, and my great ocean appears. The waves are roaring, calming, while at the same time they are smooth and calm with their deep, thundering baritone voice that is so soothing. I open all the windows and doors, except for the front entrance door. I keep it the door closed now so that I can rest undisturbed. I put my feet up to cool off. I hope that no one comes around to the ocean side to see that the door is open, and my feet are up on the sofa. I fall asleep, lulled by the repetitive chorus of the waves.

There is some small food that was prepared yesterday. I awaken and I heat it up, then, sitting at the table on the veranda, I eat while the crow walks along my fence looking longingly up at his home in the coconut tree. I wonder if his wife put him out of the nest! I sometimes see them squabbling in the early mornings. He flies off and lands among the sticky cactus leading down to the rocky beach.

After I have my fill of dinner, I put my feet up and watch the waves. I see dipping below the waves, there are tiny, glimmering lights. There it is! Opps! It's gone! There it is again! These are my fishermen in their hand carved, wooden boats. They are my friends whom I see every morning. Now their work has begun for the long night at sea. The ocean changes colors as the sun descends quickly over the horizon. Darkness comes rapidly! There is no long, slowly changing rainbow sky. The sun goes down. Bloop! It's dark!

Every night I sit on the veranda, listening to the waves. I sit in the dark. Half the time it is by choice. Sometimes I go inside to turn on the lights, sometimes it is *"lights off"* and there is no light anywhere in the neighborhood. Often, I don't turn the lights on because that would disturb my prayer. The ocean soothes my mind. She gives me messages of peace, salvation, forgiveness and

34

understanding. She knows all, and She receives all into Her bosom. I sleep. Sometimes I awaken late in the night and find my way to the bed. *"Lights off"* nights are eleven hours long. I sleep, and then the rooster begins again.

My Life is a Meditation.

Cottage by the sea.

Paper Dolls

Ayensudu-Brenu-Akymin, Ghana

I remember my first attempt to squeeze my true self into a pattern acceptable the wider community – especially my biological family. I had birthed my first daughter *'out of wedlock'*. I still had a relationship with her father. We traveled together to see my mother; I proudly showed off my newborn. Her father was a Blackfoot-Osage Indian from Oklahoma, whom I met at a Black Panther house in San Francisco.

He was not exactly the type of man my family expected me to marry. He had only a high school education, but he was a skilled hunter, marksman and horseback rider. In my final attempt to become *'acceptable'* to my family I engaged in a marriage of convenience to a highly educated distinguished and professional man who gave me a *'Mrs.'* and my children a father.

Before meeting him, I had spent most of my adult life alone as a single parent; I was in pursuit of the spiritual meanings in life. I was a person with a true mission, i.e., to rise to heights of cosmic consciousness and spiritual enlightenment. This was not just a desire or an intellectual pursuit – it was a true calling. This was reflected in my recorded dreams, my poetry, my readings, meditations, daily activities and writings. I was on a definite road to finding my true spiritual self.

Marriage, wifery and motherhood soon took me away from my direct path and I found myself using the knowledge and

36

skills that I had acquired in my spiritual quests in furtherance of the desires and ambitions of my mate. Like clothing for paper dolls, I cut myself into fragments and pieces and dressed my mate in the fashions of his ambitions. It took twenty-seven years before I realized that I was naked and my '*self*' no longer existed. I was lost, defrocked and fully '*spent*'.

I did not know how to retrieve my identity because I saw myself '*trapped*' in a financial dependency. I was angry at myself for allowing my spirit to be stifled and I was afraid to venture out on my own as I had done in my youth. The material world of '*needs*' had captured my spirit of independence and free will. I doubted my innate knowledge that all things are provide when I walk on the path of my true self toward my '**Divine Mission**'.

To find my own mind and heart again it took another seven years to restore myself to the singular path to spiritual attainment. I spent three of these years in Mother Africa planting *Moringa* trees. The first of these seven years were spent in mental torment. I could not identify my real problem – that I had clothed the body of someone else. The realization came abruptly from that person when he revealed to me that those paper doll cut-outs, those pieces of myself – my talents and knowledge that he wore so proudly and so arrogantly displayed, really did belong to him and I had no right to claim them. It was then that I knew for sure that my soul had been robbed and my spirit was naked!

In a desperate move to save my life I left all my belongings and traveled to Ghana. Within days of my arrival an oceanside cottage fell into my hands. I spent most days gazing into the water, watching the fishing boats, the sun rising, the moon rising, the clouds, the waves, the rain, the vultures, the lizards and the black and white crows. It was the ocean's movements that calmed me and began to mend my fragmented spirit. Long days and long nights, together with my laptop, I examined my heart and my mind in an attempt to understand where I was and what I needed to do.

As long as I can remember I have cared deeply about the condition of others, my people and the greater humanity. My inner being cringed and personally '*hurt*' deeply when I witnessed man's inhumanity and the human species' disregard for Mother Earth. I spent hours communicating with friends and associates – old and new – who became my internet community. I followed news developments in the USA while I observed daily routines in Ghana. It was through these activities that I regained my sense of self, who I really am. The mission that was assigned to me in 1993 by the Ethiopian Prophet, Kasa, was embraced again.

My family purchased a large plot of land in Ghana and I began to plant Moringa trees. The more trees I planted the stronger I became and the closer I felt to my own inner self – the eternal part of me that I had abandoned. Through my writings, my communications with myself and the Great Spirit – and anyone else who would listen, I slowly recaptured parts of my soul that had served as paper doll '*cut-outs*' for others.

My years of study and training in metaphysics, world religions, natural sciences, food sciences, natural medicine, herbal medicine, world history, African history, plant sciences, horticulture, astronomy and astrology found a useful outlet on the Moringa farm. **Moringa oleifera** is the Biblical *'Tree of Life'*, the *'Miracle Tree of Hope'* the mystical nurturer of the traumatized human race – my people. For the healing of the nations I shall spend my many joyful senior days placing seeds of the Miracle tree in the soil of many nations and teach them how to use it. I am content.

Feb 2, 2010

Light Bodies, the Harmonic Concordance

and the Tree of Life

"The Virgin, depicted in the constellations as Virgo, represents the Garden, Harvests and the Tree of Life. This constellation explains why humanity must undergo incarnation in the physical form, must work and struggle, have pain and hardships and go through other experiences. Without these experiences humanity could not acquire the knowledge and power which enables them to participate in divine attributes; because man and woman are made in the image of God.

Virgo represents the descent of the soul into matter. Mother Earth is the place of the soul's gestation. After the soul has partaken of the Tree of Good and Evil it can be re-born into a more glorious life."

Mama Kali's Journal -- March 3, 2003

I wrote these words several months before the *Harmonic Concordance* of November 8-11, 2003. This rare astrological event represented a moment of balance, unity, beauty, peace and power when the planets aligned to create a six-pointed star, the Star of David, two interlocking triangles in the sky in the Water signs of Cancer, Scorpio and Pisces and in the Earth signs of Taurus, Virgo and Capricorn.

This was a time for cleansing when there was a rip, *a tear or hole in the fabric of Time* that appeared to those who prepared themselves to walk through the hole and take on a luminous body. This was the time of the closing out of a "dimension", a wormhole caused by magnetic fields that first opened at the

40

"Philadelphia Experiment" in 1943.

On October 26, 2003, thirteen days before the *Harmonic Concordance* I awakened with the following dream; I recorded the dream in my journal.

5:22 AM Eastern Standard Time (Daylight Savings changed this morning)

Dream: *We went to the ocean where we sat on some high rock. Several people were there. I caught a fish and put it live into a small container that had the shape of a fish. Another lady caught a crab.*

As some people were leaving one man said that I was a threat. He was sitting higher on the rock and began to descend. I asked him why I posed a treat. He would not answer. His friend who was sitting higher on the rock still said that I was radiating light. That is why I posed a threat.

Many of the people joined in. They all agreed that I was radiating light but they did not feel that I was a threat. My partner said that we should leave. As we began to pack our things, one lady and man asked me to give a speech or sermon to vindicate myself, or to put everyone at ease. I awakened to the sound of thunder. The rain began.

[End of Dream]

Two days ago I uncovered this journal as I was cleaning a room in my house that I deserted five years before. Many of my personal things were just where I left them. I cannot say exactly what happened around that time, but it is certain that I still had some difficult earthly lessons to learn prior to my time to adorn my luminous body. As I have shared so much of my personal trials and tribulations with all of you, my pain and my sorrows, these experiences were absolutely necessary for my soul growth.

It is time for me to emerge from this dungeon and take on that **Divine Mission.** Interestingly, the last three years of my life were spent cultivating the Tree of Life (*Moringa oleifera*, aka *Nebedaye*) in the Ghana, West Africa. Immersing myself with our Great Mother Earth by cultivating the plant which is spoken of in Genesis (*the beginning*), Exodus (*the time of hardships and tribulations*) and Revelation (*the time of transcendence and transformation*), I now understand why all these personal trials were necessary.

Even as past circumstances offered unstable footing and challenging, tough obstacles, this was the time to cultivate a high moral character. Whatever events I attracted into my life it is now possible to transform them into genuine values for my soul growth.

Revelation 2:10

"Fear none of those things which thou shall suffer; behold the devil shall cast some of you into prison, that ye may be tried; and ye shall have tribulations ten days; be thou faithful unto death, and I will give you a Crown of Life."

I will move forward to take on this *"Mission"* which was prophesied by the Prophet Kasa from the high mountains of Ethiopia in June of 1993 (See: *Biblical Manna – A Spiritual Message for the New Millennium*). Prophet Kasa said that the Aboriginal women born outside of the African continent, in the African and Aboriginal Diaspora, would lead the people to salvation. My *"Mission"* is to begin to plant the Tree of Life, **Moringa oleifera**, throughout the African continent and in all the lands where the twelve tribes of Israel (Aboriginal people) are scattered. Other Aboriginal women in the Diaspora have been given other *"Missions"* which we see manifest around us each day.

Our **G.E.N.E.S.I.S.** Project was conceived and designed to proliferate throughout Africa and the Aboriginal Diaspora. G.E.N.E.S.I.S. (*Growing Energy & Nutrition for Environmental Stability & Investments in our Societies*) is a Model for providing food and energy security in rural communities, while making available to them money-making agricultural products that can be sold on the international marketplace. Using this Model can reverse the unstable food supply, poor nutrition while providing the people with improved health, environmental sustainability, and preserving their land and its biodiversity in these at risk communities. We hope that our women will join us in making this happen.

9:38 PM Eastern Daylight Time June 4, 2009

43

Red Moon Rising in Scorpio

May, 2007

This is my first time to be at this place to witness this event. On the veranda of my ocean front cottage, on the eve of the full moon, I witness this phenomenon, the full moon rising red over the equatorial Atlantic Ocean. At my one year anniversary in Ghana, this is the first time that I sat on the veranda to actually see the moon rising. For one, the moon is just beginning to rise in the southern sky, hence over the ocean where it is in my clear vision. In the past, even though I have sat on the veranda on the nights of the full moon, by the time the moon clears the coastal mountains of the northern sky, it is high in the sky, and I could never witness the color changes of the rising moon.

I notice that the moon is clearly rising between the coastal landmass and the single oil rig, whose red light always signals its presence on the dark seas of numerous nights. Today, I saw that oil rig during the daylight hours, as I traveled toward **Saltpond**, to attend an organizing meeting for female farm workers. Previously, I was told of the existence of this off-shore oil rig, and that, indeed, the red light was its signal. Never had I seen the oil rig so clearly with my own eyes, as I witnessed this day.

The decision was made several weeks ago, to replace the male farm workers with the female farm workers. I have threatened several times to release all of the male farm workers, as they have become very lax; they have now reached the point where they are just plain lazy. They come to the farm to laugh

44

and joke and get paid, all while pretending to be working. Easy money, they call it.

Now that the farm has reached critical mass, and must show something for all the hours and financial investment that has transpired, we can no longer tolerate nonsense, waste and apathy. When testing the waters for any new venture, especially with human labor, you must first test the strength, reliability, honesty and integrity of the local staff which constitutes the core experimental labor pool. I was not happy, even after the first three weeks, to see the original staff flounder, relax and get paid. Always, my philosophy is to *"give a person enough rope to hang himself."* When the execution hour arrives, the person knows why he is *"sacked"*.

Village elders pleaded with me to give the men another chance, which I did, again with the same result. The pleading and the accommodation has also reached its end, and the final chapter is written. There is a chief in another village, who told me that he only hires female farm labor. Now I know why.

At the meeting with the women, the terms of the employment and wages were discussed. As a woman, I could not bare to suggest that the women work for less than the men. However, I suggested a scheme, an age old community development and self-help financial system, where communities help each other. Here in Ghana it is called *"sui-sui"*. For each day's labor, each woman will invest approximately 16% of her wages to a common pot. When the money accumulates in the saving account, the bulk will be given to one of the women, who have shown an interest in developing a local business that will stimulate the local economy and/or add value to a locally produced product. Of course, as we move along, the women will decide exactly how the first persons who receive the *"pot"* will be selected.

These types of community based financial schemes are most honorably adhered to, more so than bank loans, because the status of the family, the honesty and integrity of the family in that community, is at stake. I have heard that in certain indigenous communities, where financial plans such as *"sui-sui"* are practiced, the recipient would rather die than to disappoint the community. They must stay true to the plan, and continue to pay into it, especially after they have received the pot.

The women and the organizers of the meeting all liked the plan, and thought that it is fair and reasonable. One of the organizers, a school teacher in another village, joked that he might quite his job to join the women at the farm. We agreed on another organizing meeting for the women, prior to the starting date.

The red moon rising in the constellation of Scorpio has concerned me. First of all, according to many of the old almanacs, a red moon portends war! Scorpio is the house of finances; it is also the house of death and transformations. This speculation of war is even more acute in my observations, because there have been two visible eclipses of the sun and the moon over Africa, and Ghana, over the past year. The total eclipse of the sun happened in March of 2006. I was not on the continent at that time. However, I have witnessed the partial eclipse of the sun over

Ghana during the month of October.

The people of Ghana are peace lovers; in fact they are peaceful to a fault, and this seemingly civil asset tends to work to their disadvantage. The people are self-sacrificing to a point of weakness. For this reason they are easily victimized especially by their former colonial masters whom they look upon as gods, being the sons and daughters of their lord and savior, Jesus Christ.

Therefore, the war I see in Ghana is a war against the people, to further victimize them and relieve them of their natural resources, the gold, diamonds, bauxite, gas, oil, timber, fisheries and agricultural crops. The most tragic war I see on the horizon is the recruitment of the young people into the armies of the United States and Britain, with a promise of citizenship to them after they serve a certain time. The young people do not know that they will be recruited to fight a *"war on terror"* where there is no identifiable enemy or specific place of abode of the army of that enemy. In other words, these innocent young men and women are desperately seeking a way out of their own homes. They see no rescue from what they believe to be poverty and despair. They will be *"pawns, fodder and hostages"* to the one super power, USA and her mother, Great Britain.

I sincerely pray that in the case of Ghana, and Africa as a whole, that last years' eclipse does not portend drought. Many of the old almanacs predict such natural disasters as this over the places where the eclipse was visible. Of course, there can not be any such blanket statement to cover such a vast continent, with more than fifty nations, each with its own karmic destiny. Other

47

factors must influence the final outcome, and the drought could very well pass over this continent.

I believe in the *Great Spirit*, the Creator, the Almighty, Omnipotent, Omniscient, Omnipresent, Welder of all visible things, and Weaver of all things invisible. I believe that this *One-on-High* hears the prayers of the faithful, and responds to their needs expediently. I know that the pure prayer of the people will be known to the *One-on-High*, and protection from the *"plague"* will be granted. Those portended evil natural disasters will *"pass over"* Mother Africa, and Her people will rise up in Praises to their own ancestors, who have always been with them, even as they were abandoned and replaced by *"false gods"* and *"idols"* that represent a religion that was given to them by their European colonialists.

May the Great Spirit Bless Our People, and shine that Holy Light onto their path, that they may be guided by truth, reason, and realism.

Photo by Charles Crawford

Full moon rises over the ocean.

Full Moon in Aquarius

Somehow I feel lost, separated, alone. This is not my usual state of consciousness. I find myself alone in the midst of many who are jubilating. There is a festival going on, and many are here in Ghana, seeing Africa for the first time. I have been happy to welcome so many new faces, so many guests. But there is a damper on my face.

As the moon rose beautifully over the sea last night, casting a wide glow on the water, I was depressed by the presence of someone who somehow makes me sad far too often. He was acting in his usual way, demanding, obnoxious, arrogant and unreasonable. He was demanding that I talk to my daughter about her attitude. He was in total denial that he was guilty of any of his own accusations. I am not in the habit of hurling fictitious accusations at anyone. There is no reason for me to do that. I have no vested interest in destroying anyone's image, credibility or accusing anyone falsely.

The man just refuses to face the truth about himself, and he throws threats and hurls intimidation's at me, with the end attempt to silence me. With his visits coming too often to Ghana, I am beginning to feel crowded and limited, and the freedom that I was enjoying is beginning to be stifled. His presence is oppressive, and I am beginning to feel like a caged bird.

I have invested too much in this farm and in growing the *Moringa*. I will not be happy to pull up my roots again to move away. But I can not be treated this way again. Freedom cries out to me. Things must change. *Life is too short to live under a dark cloud.*

23 ½ ° South Latitude –

Tropic of Capricorn

She rose slowly from the dark sea. Her color was a rich, deep amber. I watched, paying close attention to every detail, and I noticed that She had a very serious face. As She climbed rapidly from the watery tomb, Her color changed, fading from the amber, slowly to a deep, daisy yellow, paler, paler and then She wore the color of real vanilla ice cream. She was the Full Moon in Capricorn.

In all Her serious face, She wore a calm beauty. I knew Her, because I learned from Her in my early days. As a young adult, I understood that life, to be successful, had to be trained in self discipline, to fully contemplate to know and understand. Within life's journeys there is joy, there is laughter, there are tears and there is discipline. To meet the challenges and to conquer your own karmic destiny, there must be self discipline.

This challenge remains the greatest - to conquer the Self. Many things can be conquered; the easiest is to conquer materialism. What we really need materially are air, water, food, clothing and shelter. These are the only physical requirements. If you are blessed to live in a tropical climate, the clothing and shelter needs are minimal. Once the desire for material things is conquered, your needs are few, and your spirit has a certain freedom. To conquer the Self is still the challenge. I have come a long way on this path but my journey is not over.

What is the greatest sacrifice of the Self? Is it to give of your

Self to a cause, a people or a world? Think of our great ones, like Grade *Nannie* of Jamaica, *Fannie Lou Haimer* of America, *Yaa Asantewaa* of Ghana, Marcus Garvey, *Kwame Nkrumah* and Martin Luther King. They were called to the ultimate sacrifice, to give of their Self to the greater cause. In all these examples, the cause was for the freedom and liberation of their people. Each did their part, and the world will never forget them. The **Powers of Darkness** continue to hold sway over this Earth, and the struggle continues.

I was sharing the beauty of this full moon in Capricorn with a young friend, a 14 year old boy from the village. When I said that the moon was at Her lowest point, he did not understand; so I sent him to the map of Africa on my living room wall.

"Find the equator; it is at zero degrees latitude." That was easy, because Ghana is very close to the equator. I then directed him to look to the south of the equator, and look for 23 ½° latitude; that is the Tropic of Capricorn.

"Now, tell me what countries does this Tropic of Capricorn cross?" The boy looked and he called off the names, South Africa, Mozambique (he had trouble pronouncing this name), Madagascar. I went further to explain that the earth moves in such a way as to create seasons, i.e., winter, spring, summer and autumn, and that the highest point that the Sun reaches is at the Summer Solstice, 23 ½° north latitude; that is the Tropic of Cancer. The lowest point that the Sun reaches is 23 ½° south latitude; that is the Tropic of Capricorn.

I told the young student that the weather begins to get cold once you pass the 30° latitude. So we went to the world map to see. The world map was purchased from a street hawker in Accra, the capital city of Ghana. I paid ¢15,000 (in 2007) for it, about $1.55. I asked the student to bring me my glasses so that I could show him the 30° latitude on the world map. I looked and looked, and I discovered that the map was wrong! WRONG!! WRONG!!!

The latitudes were numbered incorrectly, and the 60° latitude, moving through northern Canada, Northern Russia, Norway and Sweden was marked 30°. Now, I know that Jackson, Florida is near the 30° latitude, but the hawkers on the streets of Ghana are selling a map that places the 30° latitude across the coldest part of Europe and America.

I assumed that this was a criminal act! To sell dis-information and incorrect sciences (geography) is a crime! But even this is a small problem. Look at the confusion it will bring to the young minds who are studying this map, thinking that they are gaining correct knowledge. The Powers of Darkness have stooped, even to this level, to maintain their dominance. They will sell anything to unsuspecting Africans. Yet, who is there to stop them? Many of the Accra street hawkers are illiterate – most can read and count, perhaps enough to move through their daily activities. But to them each sale that they make brings them closer to earning their daily food.

It is on this day, when the Full Moon has reached Her lowest point that I realized that the greatest discipline, the greatest sacrifice is of your Self to a Cause Greater than the Self. It is a call to the sacrifice of the Self for the advancement of the People.

Post Script-- August 27, 2022.

I am just beginning to publish all these short stories that were written 15 years ago. Perhaps I was not aware that maps can be different from other cultures. I assumed that this map was wrong, but numbering the latitudes can be different. One can avoid the North South latitude confusion by giving a different value to each latitude. It does make sense, but that does not change the fact that many products sold on the streets of Africa are inferior. Many products sold in the markets of America and other so called *"civilized nations"* are also inferior. This is a FACT!

Occult – Full Moon in Pisces

She was playing hide-and seek with me, dancing about beyond the clouds, peeping from behind every now and then. At first I did not see her, for she masked her entry from behind the bosom-shaped rock jutting out of the ocean just a few feet away from my veranda. But I saw her light, shining with a silvery glitter on the calm waves of the nighttime sea. For a long time I sat waiting to see her, but she was occult, hidden, invisible, and I only knew she was there because of the silvery glow reflected on the fronds of the coconut palms. She emerged as the mermaid of the deep waters, the full moon in Pisces.

In prehistoric and ancient Egyptian days the sea was known as Uati; she is known as Mame Wata all over West Africa today. She is the one who brought forth all creation from the dark void of the celestial sea. Nun and Nuanet were the architects who ruled over the chaos and brought order from the roaring waters. In western mythology this god of the deep waters Neptune who is associated with the constellation of Pisces, a Greek male deity, who rules over the waters.

Pisces is the last constellation of the zodiac, that background of stars that define our Sun's yearly trek on the superhighway along the Milky Way. Pisces defines the evolution of the oldest human life on earth, the first people to walk upright, create languages, to cultivate crops and to develop the greatest civilization which flourished on the African and American continents, in the Nile Valley; first from the Ethiopia highlands through Sudan in what was known as Upper Egypt, down

56

through eastern Africa towards the Mediterranean which was known as Lower Egypt. The American continent developed simultaneous, or as Thoth reveals in *The Emerald Tablets of Thoth,* America was a part of *Atlantis,* which disappeared in the Great Flood, and that the great civilization of *Atlantis* was then brought to the African continent by Thoth, aka Djehuti, Tehuti.

Pisces corresponds to a state of human development where the road diverges in two paths, as embodied by the two fish of Pisces swimming in opposite directions.

Pisces symbolizes the possibilities of mankind reaching the highest spiritual attainment; on the opposite end, it represents the lowest level to which the spirit can descend into the deepest darkest regions of the mind and the soul. Pisces represents the height the soul can reach through pure worship, enlightenment, good works, and devotion to the uplifting of humanity.

Pisces can take you to the darkest regions of the soul, through drugs, alcohol, insanity, illusions, self-deception, self-abnegation and spiritual enslavement.   Pisces represents true spiritual freedom for the souls that have completed their sojourn on this planet, having accomplished the tasks set for that spirit's *Self Realization.* Pisces can also bring entrapment in a realm that is called by Christians, purgatory, the never ending, burning flames of hell. Pisces is the road of *Self-Realization* or *Self-Undoing.*

The women of this Motherland, who along with Aboriginal American women, carry the mitochondrial DNA of the original women, have reached this level in our evolution. We have a choice to make. Will we choose *Self-Realization*, the hard, tough road of devotion, to live by the *42 Principles of Ma-at*, or will we choose spiritual enslavement, through the worship of false idols, false gods by continuing to hold fast to the Piscean Age religions, Judaism, Christianity and Islam?

It is clear that at this point in history, these religions are at the heart of the self-undoing, the destruction of this planet, this world, because on every continent there is an endless war being waged in the name of one or all of these religions. Is it the people, or is it the religions? The people create the religions to mask their personal desires, and to promote their own agendas. None are about saving souls. They speak about it, but none of them practice what they speak. If the hearts of any of the leaders of any or all of these religions are placed on a scale of Justice, and weighed against a feather, like at the final judgment according to the ancient religions of the Nile, the scale would tumble. Few rabbis, few preachers, few priests, few imams could meet the test.

The Piscean religions say that your name would be in the great book, when you come knocking at the gate on Judgment Day. Their names would not appear in any book, and their hearts could not meet the feather test.

So we have a choice. Yes, we have been left a set of rules to live by. Over the past 2000 years the religions of the Piscean Age gave us **Ten Commandments**. These same religions have robbed, murdered, raped, rampaged, and assaulted the peoples of the world and our *Divine Mother Earth*, Herself, in the nameof *saving savage souls.*

There are 101 principles to guide us toward living a life of civility and living a just existence. These were given to us in the ancient teachings of the Nile Valley. There are 42 principles defined in **Ma-at**, to live in balance with Nature, with justice, embracing mercy, in accordance with peace, in concerted harmony and compassion; this is the sacred road to enlightenment. If we follow these principles, we will swim in the direction of pure ecstasy and spiritual freedom. We will follow the Piscean fish into the *Celestial River of Eridanus,* the Sea of Immortality.

Baby Boy

John Singleton's 2001 movie

"...a Afrikan man irretrievably caught in total whiteness, is humanity at its most destroyed. He knows his disease; the only cure he knows is the disease itself intensified." from: **Why Are We So Blest?**

By Ayi Kwei Armah

Baby Boy in Africa

I continue to be concerned and confused about the state of the Aboriginal American man child. This quote was sent by email to me by Akoben House in Georgia. The founder quotes one of my favorite authors, Ayi Kwei Armah, a Ghanaian national who has written some of the most moving historical novels in recent times (i.e., **Two Thousand Seasons**, **The Healers**, **The Beautiful Ones are Not Yet Born**). Little did I know that, within days of receiving this quote from my Brother, I would experience first hand a prime example of such an Aboriginal man who is caught up in total whiteness. My experience with this person over the past ten days here in Ghana left me drained, and almost on the brink of a nervous breakdown.

A long time friend in America asked that we guide her son through the process of a business start up in Ghana. The son is 33 years old, a graduate of a high ranking historical Negro college with advanced degrees from America's elite Ivy League schools. The son's former work was in space age technology. He is divorced, with a 10-year-old son whom he doesn't see very often. He is the third or fourth generation of a well-to-do professional Aboriginal family. We never met this young man before his arrival in Ghana; however, we have known his mother for several years. We have heard no mention of the young man's father from anyone.

From the time of his arrival at the airport we knew that something was not quite right; but we did not jump to conclusions. We spent several days taking him around and introducing him to Ghanaians who could guide him in his chosen profession. I had a chance to talk to him about many topics as we traveled from cities to towns to villages in Ghana. It was apparent that his upbringing was privileged, suburban and white. His bachelor's degree from a historical Negro college did not give him much exposure to Aboriginal American history and extraordinarily little African history. Although his mother named him after a great Pan African and African president, his education and exposure did not live up to or prepare him for the name.

This young Aboriginal American entrepreneur had made several attempts to launch his business prior to meeting us; all attempts had failed and had resulted in big financial losses. His mother and grandmother, however, were still willing to financially support his efforts to break into this business despite the previous heavy losses. It did not take long for us to see why his efforts had failed.

1. He attempted to start up and follow the business and make contacts over the internet
2. He believed whatever story the internet sellers told him
3. He did not weigh the validity of their claims nor investigate their background or their official businesses

61

status

4. He did not investigate the individuals before making financial and material commitments, even though he claimed that he was thorough at scrutinizing the sources prior to commencing business

Observing his behavior over several days alerted me to the fact that he was careless, reckless, and unprofessional. He would make business calls in hotel lobbies and talk loudly so that everyone could hear. This made people aware that the business he was engaged in meant that he must have money in his pocket. He was careless with his wallet. This placed him in danger of being robbed, and it took no time before his wallet was lifted. We took him to the office that issues licenses for people engaged in the business that he was interested in. We found that two of his internet sources were known by the licensing office because of their questionable business practices. In spite of this knowledge the young man still wanted to do business with one of these people, even though we laid the groundwork for him to proceed along a legal pathway with legitimate Ghanaian dealers.

Over the days we moved together the young man's behavior became more and more irrational. We could not talk sense to him. He was in frequent contact with his mother and grandmother. The mother and grandmother also continued to talk with us, urging us to stay with the young man until he completed the business deal that we set in place for him.

It was a difficult chore. When an adult behaves like

a child you cannot prevent them from hurting themselves. I was on the brink of a nervous breakdown watching this grown man self-destruct; there was nothing I could do. When he insisted on staying in the capitol city to continue to do business with a person whose reputation was questionable, we could not stay with him. He was determined to do what he wanted to do.

Baby Boy in Africa; he is a spoiled brat, yet physically a grown man. He was not grounded in knowledge of self. He did not read books written by African scholars on African history. He did not read books by Aboriginal American scholars about Aboriginal American history. He did not read psychology and sociology books written by people of African descent. He was schooled in *"whiteness"* and he pursued *"whiteness"*. **"Whiteness"** has almost destroyed him; he is riddled in the disease of *"whiteness"*.

He was apparently spoiled by his mother and grandmother. I don't know what role his father played. I have seen this scenario play over and over again. Too many Aboriginal women spoil their sons while they raise their daughters. I see this happening also in Ghana. The girls work from a very young age, learning to take care of the boys and men. The boys and men sit under a tree, talk religion and politics, play soccer and dominoes, watch athletic games on TV and drink.

When will we stop this mad dash to self destruction? Our greatest hope is self knowledge, but instead of learning about our own suffering, our own greatness, our own achievements both past and present; instead of creating our own future, we blindly follow the laid down processes that contribute to the continuing goals of "white supremacy", all this to our own self-destruction. (See: **The Falsification of African Consciousness** by Dr. Amos Wilson)

If we can help this 33-year-old man at this point in life, I cannot say. But we can help those coming along right now. The Beautiful Ones ARE born NOW! They are the Indigo children, born from 1990's until this day. They are our own children, our own grandchildren. We can direct them and give them those tools they need to break away from "*whiteness*". "**Whiteness**" is their disease; "*whiteness*" is their plague. But all that they know is "*whiteness*".

The cure for this disease is self-knowledge; the cure for this disease is self-reliance; the cure for this disease is self-sufficiency. This information is available for all of us who want to know and who are willing to accept responsibility and change, Change, CHANGE from our own hands and under our exclusive dictates and directions.

- All we have to do is open the books!
- All we have to do is begin to use our unique creative talents for our own benefit and for our own future.
- All we have to do is realize that the riches of the world in ALL respects were given to Aboriginal people.
- All we have to do is to realize that we are the **Original Americans**

- All we have to do is to develop the vast riches that were bestowed upon our land in the US and US alone.
- All we have to do is learn to Love Ourselves!!

"WE ARE THE ONES WE HAVE BEEN WAITING FOR!!"

Thank you for this quote
Sista June Jordan

Baby Girl in America
Response to Baby Boy

Amen from Coco in Washington, D. C.

I overstand your comments and concerns! We are the ONES we have been waiting for. All we have to do is accept the responsibility and the glory will come. I am so happy this young sister spent time with you when she was in Ghana.

On a high note, Baby Girl was at my house for two months while attending her internship at the National Institute of Health. Our young budding scientist and alternative healing doctor studied Moringa with you and brought all her knowledge with her to NIH. She had outstanding results as she scientifically tested Moringa on cancerous cells. Her results were so powerful that many interested people showed up to hear her findings at the poster review process with her final project. Of course, there was a lot of press present and many other scientists. Please contact her and get control of this information for use with our people as soon as possible. You KNOW that they will use this information and capitalize on her study for THEIR benefit.

Since you have known this information for sooooo long, your own efforts can only be enhanced by using and spreading he good news she was able to study and reveal just recently. She returned to California last weekend and can still be reached by phone. Don't wait too long; you know that the race belongs to the swift, and the next thing you know *Moringa* will be selling all over the place, and they will figure out a way to shut you out of the business. It's the American way. Go for it!

Sincerely, Coco

*PS By the time I returned to America and got in touch with Baby Girl, Moringa was on everybody's tongue. But that wasn't all. There was a European woman who was the head of a non-profit organization N.G.O. in Ghana who sent one of her Ghanaian **spies** to snoop to see what we were doing with Moringa and report back to her. Before we knew what was happening there were posters on street corners in Amsterdam with a very dark-skinned man holding a European baby and advertising Moringa.*
Mama Kali

Upward Mobility Creates Apathy in Aboriginal Americans

Upward mobility, trying to *"make it"* in Apartheid America, demands that those who are "upward bound" in the socioeconomic realm cannot, or will not find the time to look critically at where they are headed in their search to *"make it"* or whether through their intense activities connecting to this mobility, they will actually get to where they think they want to be when they finally decide that they *"made it"*.

What I mean by all these words, is that Aboriginal Americans are so busy working at "moving on up" that they don't see where they are going, or whether this will be their "final answer" or "final destination", that place or position that, when they get there, it fulfills their deepest desire of mind, heart, and spirit. I have yet to see an Aboriginal person who was happy because they thought that they had *"made it"*. What I have seen is individuals who continue to strive to become more "qualified" or "accepted" or more "acceptable" to the larger community. Whenever they "get there", they find themselves isolated from their own families and communities and taunted by their colleagues or the media for every tiny infraction or lapse in judgment. They are *"targets"* and serve as *"scapegoats"* for almost any personal weakness of social impropriety.

This is obvious in the case of almost any Aboriginal celebrity. The media finds a way to blame Aboriginal celebrities for all of American society's sins. The cases are too numerous to point out. All of us can site at least three cases where Aboriginal celebrities have taken the blame for what almost all celebrities dowhether it is illegal enhancement drugs, street drugs, soliciting prostitutes or same sex relationships or just back yard animal fights. I am not saying that any of these activities are good. Others in this society do the same things, yet the media acts as if it is something peculiar to only Aboriginal people. I have said for many years that Aboriginal people are blamed for white people's sins.

Aboriginal people are now blamed for slavery, as we have recently seen at the 200th anniversary of the ending of slavery by the British here in Ghana. I personally witness the fiasco that was presented at the Castle at Elmina, Ghana at the celebration of the 200th Anniversary of the Abolition of Slavery by the British. The President of Ghana actually stood up before everyone to admit that the British were really not to blame for slavery. This is another story that I will share at another time. This practice of Africans owning up to slavery continues without end. It is known as *"blaming the victim"*.

In Aboriginal intelligentsia, I see our people continue to strive to earn more letters behind their names. I have yet to see those who have moved upward to the level of international recognition as an *"authority"* on the subject, unless they have learned to quote word for word what their *"master"* told them to say. Independent thinkers are never recognized by the established order, and they are never given a larger national or international stage. Aboriginal historians are only widely recognized in Aboriginal communities. I have actually seen many books where white people use Aboriginal historians' research and information without giving them credit. This happens on every professional level, from computer science to medicine and advanced scientific research, including mathematics and physics.

In the business world it is the same. Here in Ghana, I had a debate with a learned Aboriginal American professional woman. It was about the Aboriginal CEO of a major international corporation based in New York City. I saw an interview where this CEO was uplifted by an Aboriginal historian as one whom we should aspire to immolate.

Although it is commendable that he attained this position, I personally saw him as a *"put-butt."* He spoke about how he had to dance around the white guys at his *"white only"* country club and golf course. He said that he didn't want them to be *"afraid of him"*, so he was careful to act and behave with a false humility and in a self-effacing manner. I wonder what white man in the same position, a corporate president, would behave in such a way. The white man would surely act in an arrogant and self-assured, perhaps even a boastful manner, and the white men around him would respect his behavior.

In my opinion, this CEO has not *"made it"* because he is still begging for acceptance from those whom he should have no concern as to whether they like him or not. After all, he probably holds a higher position than most of the white guys at the country club, those whom he is begging to be their friend. I'm sure they laugh at him when his back is turned. As for apathy, when was the last time that this Aboriginal CEO went to a lecture on Aboriginal history, or pulled out a book by an Aboriginal author in front of his white colleagues.

Would he bring his white colleagues up to date on Aboriginal inventors and other noted Aboriginal achievers? I would bet all my worldly possessions that he would die before he did that. In fact, I'm certain that he does his best to stay abreast of what THEY are reading, and hence, he never gets to know the truth about himself and his real status in Apartheid America.

If he has any relationship with any Aboriginal folks, it is probably at church, if he goes to one. Aboriginal folks usually go to Aboriginal churches, even if they have to drive 20 miles to find one. There, in the Aboriginal church he is treated like a *"rock star"* and among the parishioners he certainly maintains the arrogance of the one who *"made it"*.

In order to maintain his position in the white professional community, he cannot pretend to be aware of or concerned about the happenings in the Aboriginal community. Hence, he pretends that he doesn't care. After a while, because he is so removed from the Aboriginal community and the truth of everyday life there, he becomes so entrenched in apathy that he forgets his own roots – completely. He really doesn't care anymore, or he blames the Aboriginal community for their condition

The ultimate outcome in the apathy of the *"upward bound"* Aboriginal American is the poor health that most of them experience. The stress of not being oneself, not being truthful to oneself, the stress of being an *"over-achiever"* to always strive to do better than everyone, takes a toll on one's health. Heart weakness, hypertension, and diabetes and among men, prostate diseases, among women, breast diseases and a multitude of long named psychotic conditions, are common among *"over-achievers"*. If they attain wealth, it can disappear trying to find a chemical treatment for what is really a condition of *"**not** knowing thyself"*. All the wealth, social status, professional recognition, awards and not even the white woman or white man that some of them marry, don't fill that gap. Have they *"made it"*? Have they *"arrived"*? **Questionable.**

Forgiveness: Key to Survival & Liberation

Over the last few days I have been in a deep meditation. I re-read Dr. Amos Wilson's book, The Falsification of African Consciousness. Because he so correctly identifies the psychosis that so totally grips the American and African Aboriginal consciousness, throughout the Diaspora, particularly in America. I feel compelled to share this book with everyone. I took the last two days to outline this book, and I am sharing it with you today. Although Dr. Wilson has joined the ancestors, I'm certain that he would approve of my sharing his great work in the spirit that he intended, i.e., to unlock the chains that bind us to the negative images of ourselves and a continuing under-productive lives.

The book is 140 pages long; it has been condensed to 18 pages. My wish is that you will print this document and take these 18 pages around with you, in your purse, your briefcase or your backpack, and whenever you are sitting idol, bring it out to read just a few sentences or a few paragraphs. You will come to understand your self, your family and your own motivations, hang-ups and unconscious obstacles on the road to your personal success and liberation.

It is time to get honest with ourselves. The clock is ticking, the pendulum and swinging, and if we have not confronted the negative and self destructive aspects of our selves, we will not live to see the pendulum swing up in our favor. We must remember that time favors no person, time judges all persons. The fact that we were given freedom to make personal choices and personal decisions in this garden of life gives us permission to claim our

72

time at that moment when the pendulum swings in our favor. If we fail to meet this moment in time and space, our futures are forever doomed to turn the grindstone, like a mule in the corn mill.

Many of us claim to be Christian, and the hallmark of Christianity is forgiveness. We must "forgive those who trespass against us". We manage to forgive those who have committed the most atrocious sins against us, the Europeans and Euro-Americans. But we have not forgiven our family members, our mothers, our fathers, our sisters our brothers, our aunties our uncles, our cousins, our husbands or our wives, all those whom we share a common blood or a common history through other family ties. Most of all, we must forgive ourselves. Perhaps this is the hardest thing to do, because we do not easily recognize the blame that we hold so closely and so secretly within ourselves. Please, please print this condensed version of -- The Falsification of Afrikan Consciousness. Make ten copies and share it with friends conscious enough to take the time to understand, and sincere enough to try to make needed changes. Do not caste pearls before swine (you know what I mean). If you think you are too busy to read this much, the next time you get kicked in the behind on the job or in other business relationships, or when you get physically ill because of undo stress, remember that an opportunity knocked, and you failed to take the time to open the door.

Identity

Identity for a Black (Aboriginal) man in America is a very serious issue. Gzee didn't really fit into the throng of children in his East Oakland neighborhood where he lived with his mother, a single parent divorcee who worked hard and provided a stable, safe and beautiful home for her family. He looked different and the other kids knew that he was, somehow, not quite like them. Gzee never fit in with his father's family; he didn't speak the language. And Gzee was a sensitive child; he was an artist.

Last Saturday Gzee ended his own life; I do not know what finally brought on his tragic end. He was depressed and despondent almost all the time. He joined the armed forces and was released shortly thereafter on a medical leave. He couldn't stay in college or any other formal career training. He could not keep a job. He whiled away his days playing video games and just moving around from place to place.

His mother, Renee, gave her children all the best. They were always well dressed, well feed and had the best and latest toys, video games, CD's – whatever the other kids had. Renee was a fine example of middle-class American values; she was always advancing in her job, she came home to cook and clean. She even had time for interior decorating. This was her hobby. Every home she lived in was soon a picture book of upscale design; she purchased her first home when she was in her early twenties. She always had a credit score of good to excellent, a rare achievement in the Aboriginal American community.

Gzee belonged to the generation once removed from the Black Power Movement in East Oakland. If he had been born during the Black Panther days in East Oakland perhaps he would have had a stronger self identity. There was an issue of belonging to something which held itself up, heads high with pride and dignity before the Party was brought under full attack by the FBI pogrom and program, *Cointelpro*. This attack was followed by **the invasion of drugs** into the community, especially **heroin**, which I personally witnessed in the **late 1960's**.

Gzee did not get involved in drugs or gangs or movements of any kind. No one ever knew what was on his mind. Was it identity? He looked Asian like his father, was raised in a Black community until his mother moved the family away into a white suburban community. Upward mobility, they call it. He did not look like those kids either. When Renee remarried the husband himself did not have a strong self-identity. Renee's new husband's mother was white, his father was Black and he was juggled between family and foster homes. He was a hard worker and shared the desire and longing for a beautiful home like Gzee's mother, Renee.

Last summer I met a wonderful Afro-Swiss lady here in Ghana. She is more Pan-African than most American Aboriginals that I know. She was born isolated in the Swiss Alps, hundreds of miles from any other brown-skinned person. Her mother gave her a copy of Malcolm X when she was 14 years old; this started her on a life-long study of African history. There are successful mixed raced children; most have a strong parent who guides them in some definite direction. We can name the famous ones.

"Know thyself", was first spoken by Imhotep, the Egyptian Visier, more than two thousand years before Hippocrates, the Greek. The oath that all medical doctors take is not the Hippocratic Oath but Imhotep's Oath. The Greeks changed Imhotep's name to Aslepeaius when they stole the African heritage from the Nile Valley (See *Stolen Legacy* by George G. M. James, 1954). How many doctors know that they vow to *"do no harm"* to an African genius who built the step pyramid in Egypt? How many Aboriginal doctors know this?

Did Gzee know? I regret that I was not closer to him. I have not seen him in eleven years since I moved away from San Francisco. He didn't say much the last time I saw him. It is for the salvation of young people like Gzee that we are holding the **First Grandmothers in Ghana Think Tank** here in Ghana's Central Region this summer June 30 to July 3, 2008. We can not bear to continue to loose our children, our grandchildren, our nieces and nephews to the crisis of self identity since the fall of the Civil Rights Movement and the Black Power Movement. Yes, the fall of the Civil Rights Movement and the Black Power Movement! It was never the same after the assassination of Martin Luther King and Malcolm X and Fred Hampton. Many of our people took the bribe, took the political appointment, took the job, took the education grant and tucked their pride firmly between their legs. Our pride has not yet been retrieved.

In our small Aboriginal American community here in Elmina, (where most of us believed that we are African-Americans), we have lost two of our youth. Mama Betty's

grandson was shot in the head in Michigan a few months ago. He died a few days later. Ironically Mama Betty and I were talking about organizing Grandmothers in Ghana just minutes before she got the news. Now Gzee hanged himself. We do not want to wait to see whose child will be next. Can we afford to wait, and see?

Gzee's drawing at age 11.

Insanity and the Psychosis of Oppression

Insanity -- To continue to do the same things in the same way, over and over again, and expect a different outcome.

After all the expenditures Aboriginal Americans incurred to go to Jena to protest the cruel and unusual treatment of our children, and the criminalization of our children, I can no longer wonder what ails us. We have to be **INSANE**, to believe that a 1950's protest march will cause any changes in Apartheid America!!!

The reason why the protest marches made a difference in 1950's -60's is because Apartheid America was loosing money; we *BOYCOTTED* their goods and they lost their *MOST BELOVED – MONEY!!!*

I remember attending a protest march just three years ago, after a Brother, who had done everything white folks told him to do to gain *"acceptance"*, education, professional job, home and family was shot down in cold blood in front of his friends by a Columbus, Georgia policeman. The policeman was not punished; he was rewarded with a high paying job in Iraq.

After using all the conventional channels of redress to seek justice for our Brother, everyone was frustrated and called for a protest march. I had not joined a protest march in more than twenty years, but felt compelled to join the Atlanta community on that day. My entire family joined the protest, including the grandchildren. So what happened? *NOTHING!!!*

The *Negro Disciples of White Supremacy*, who are often called *our leaders*, whose names we all recognize, decided that we should not boycott the most likely candidate, an insurance company, headquartered in Columbus that makes millions of dollars from Aboriginal Americans. As a result of no monetary losses or consequences to the city of Columbus, Georgia, there was no reason for them to consider finding justice for the slain brother.

This story is repeated over and over in Apartheid America. Are we so conditioned by our circumstances of oppression that we can no longer care to suffer a little discomfort of boycotting anything in order to realize justice for our children? It is obvious that the psychosis of oppression has gripped us in death throes. We are unable to make any changes in the way we address our oppressors; we are clutched by fear; we are under the hypnotic control of white supremacy programming. We are unable to act in our own best interest.

Where do we go from here? We must let go of the fear; that means that we must forgo desire, especially the desire for **THINGS**. We must relinquish our fear of death and retribution. *We must surrender our belief that we will be rewarded after we die.* Our reward is here and now!! We must not wait for death, because our deeds in life will stand as our judge. We will never be forgiven by God or any other Judgment for standing on the sidelines and allowing our children to be abused and misused by the powers of darkness and evil on earth.

We can not allow our children to be criminalized and remanded to the slavery of the *"Prison Industrial Complex"*. Yep, you heard it, the **Prison Industry**!! *The new slave plantation is waiting for our children*, and we are too scared to do any more than a protest march. We are too scared to boycott fast food, beer companies, cola companies, shopping mega-stores, clothing companies, shoe makers, car dealers and everything else. So we allow them to take our children away as chattel -- in 2007.

SHAME ON YOU!! So can we make a resolute change of direction? I believe that we can. I believe that the Grandmothers and Mothers must step forward, as the warrior women of Africa and the Aboriginal Diaspora have always done over the last 500 years to save our people.

I urge you to join the *Women Are Ready (W.A.R.)* We can make plans to change our direction for our survival. If you are too scared to loose your job or your white friends or your house or your car, please don't join us. *We have to* **WALK** *in* **FAITH** *and we must* **WALK** *in* **CONFIDENCE WITHOUT FEAR***!! Our* **MISSION** *is* **BLESSED** *because the* **TIME IS NOW***!!!*

Generational Male Sacrifice:

The Legacy of Colonialism and Servitude

Yesterday with the New Moon in Sagittarius and the American Holiday of Thanksgiving I watched two programs in Ghana, *"Boston Legal"* an American network television show and *"The Secret Life of Bees"*, a movie featuring three popular and talented Aboriginal American women. These were an interesting pair to ponder on a day when everyone eats too much while relaxing and with family and friends.

Both movies were about family and friends. *"The Secret Life of Bees"* was set in rural South Carolina in 1964, the year that Michelle Obama, America's new First Lady, was born. *"Boston Legal"* was set in Boston Massachusetts in 2008. The high-powered white lawyers sat around the Thanksgiving dinner table arguing about how racism has not changed and will not change just because Barack Obama was the first *"Black"* American to be elected President of the United States. There was one little Aboriginal boy at the dinner table with these racists' lawyers; he was about ten years old and he was present at the table because one of the middle aged male lawyers picked him as a pet project instead of *"fly fishing"*. (*He actually said that.*)

Before I went to bed I ran across an old diary; I decided to open it and ponder the past. There was only one entry – November 18, 1991. I had just arrived in Lagos, Nigeria with my eldest sister.

I had barely escaped extreme stress and fatigue in my home in San Francisco. My passport was stolen that night. The entry in my diary related the arrival at the airport as the typical Nigerian chaos and confusion with harassment in Customs and Immigration and the many police checkpoints along the road where my passport was passed around and handled by so many people; it was lost in the shuffle.

In that diary entry I promised myself that I would treat myself to a massage every day while I was in Lagos. I could afford that type of pampering in Nigeria, and I really needed the personal care. I was stressed to the limit with family members and family business commitments over the years. I escaped to save myself.

So, what does *"Boston Legal"* and *"The Secret Life of Bees"* have to do with Barack and Michelle Obama, generational male sacrifice, and my personal stress? The racism that we Aboriginal women have endured over the years, with the accompanying sacrifice of our male children, brothers, husbands, and fathers has culminated with the election of an *"Black"* man to lead the most powerful nation in the world. But deep down this nation has not changed.

At this time in the history of the United States the last hope of the white race lies in the promises of their redemption from the sins of their fathers; thus, Barack Obama rose to the Presidency.

How ironic it was that two days ago I bought a movie set in South Carolina in 1964. Being in Ghana for the past year I had never heard of the movie. I choose *"The Secret Life of Bees"* because of the women stars – Queen Latifah, Jennifer Hudson, Alicia Keys, and Sophie Okonedo. It was set at the height of the Civil Rights struggle and the year that President Lyndon Johnson signed the Civil Rights Act in the presence of our hero, Dr. Martin Luther King; the movie showed this historic footage.

The savagery, cruelty, evil and inhumane treatment the white people committed against the Aboriginals in the movie was extreme, and it was a true depiction. I personally witnessed their brutality and viciousness in my southern hometown during the 1960's. In the movie the whites beat both Aboriginal men and Aboriginal women to a pulp and I feared that the young boy who was beaten would turn up dead. The boy in this movie was another Aboriginal male sacrifice; his hopes and dreams were shattered along with his beaten and maimed body and spirit.

The young white girl in the movie who was rescued, nurtured, defended, loved, trained to make a living, housed, educated and protected by the Aboriginal women was played by blond haired and blue-eyed Dakota Fanning. The greatness, the loving kindness, the sincerity, and the goodness of the women made her life worth living. The little white girl may never have survived the cruelty of her biological white father if our women were not in her life. Again, we saved the whites, as we have always done throughout our history together on this American continent, the Civil War, the Spanish American War, World War I and World War II Korean War and all other wars and conflicts.

In *"Boston Legal"* the typical depiction of a dysfunctional 10 year old Aboriginal boy was a very predictable television stereotype. The fact that a middle aged, professional, single white male would adopt this child made my hair stand on end, especially since most of the male figures in the television episode seemed to have serious mental/emotional problems. I feared for the little boy, and I feared for his future. Perhaps he could be another Aboriginal male sacrifice.

So here we are at the precipice,facing an uncertain future of this great empire called America. Everyone knows that we are in the last days; no one can see how we can survive the inhumane rule of the European and American hegemony. In their arrogance they also know that they cannot continue on this destructive and selfish path of materialism and global warfare. It has reached the pivot point and it must come down. But they pray that someone can save them, and in their desperation, and in the depth of their being they know that, in the past their only salvation has been the goodness, kindness and mercy of the America's Original people.

Deborah said, *"Arise Barak and take away your captives."* [Hebrews 5:11]

Then Deborah the prophetess called Barak saying, *"Go and march to Mount Tabor, and take with you 10,000 men ..."* [Judges 4:6];

And Barak said to her, "If you will go with me then I with go; but if you do not go with me, I will not go." [Judges 4:8}

And Deborah said,

"I will surely go with you; nevertheless, the honor shall not be yours on the journey that you are about to take, for the Lord will sell Sisera (the enemy)*into the hands of a woman..."* [Judges 4:9]

And it is the women who will be our salvation -- who will save us all, as our women have saved our men over the centuries, although many Original males have been sacrificed along the way. We could not save them all. Our women, the Aboriginal American women who have labored and sacrificed, been judged and mistreated, gone unappreciated and disregarded, have given and continue to give, who have toiled and go unrewarded and who have again and again sacrificed our fathers, our brothers, our husbands, and our sons until this day of judgment – we are tired, and we need to de-stress, and we need to rest. Soon, I pray, soon.

Thus is the Decency of the Children of God, thus is the Grace of the Sons of God, thus is the Mercy of the Daughters of the Most High, thus is the Benevolence of the true Hebrews—the Aboriginal-Americans, Akan-Hebrew Israelites, thus is the Fate of our Times.

Michael Jackson

Another Male Sacrifice?

I just watched, **"This is It!"** Michael Jackson's final rehearsals of what become his last live performances. Actually, I was surprised at his energy and his unconquerable skills singing, dancing and performing. After all the propaganda after his suspicious death I though that he would look a bit frail and lifeless. But quit the opposite. Sure, he could have used at least another 20 pounds; he sure would have looked better, but with the energy necessary to perform at his level of perfection, he probably performs at his peak without all that extra weight.

I have been a Michael Jackson fan since the **Jackson Five** burst on the scene when he was six years old. I remember watching them in Black & White on the **Ed Sullivan Show**. My girls and I wore out at least two "**Off the Wall**" 33 speed records. I still have one in a box in my closet. When she first saw it, my granddaughter remarked, "**This sure is a big CD.**" At six years old, she had never seen a 33 speed record.

As we watched his moves, I pointed out to the four grandchildren some of the leg motions that were strictly "**James Brown**", and how the **Godfather of Soul** was Michael's mentor. Even the four year old now knows the words to many of Michael's songs and will soon know all the dances. He only has to see a dance move once, and he has the moves down pat!

I was so sadden to hear of Michael's death, but I knew that he was a very heartbroken man. *What the American Press did to him, to his soul and his spirit, was criminal.* I never believed any of the accusations against Michael because I really understood where he was coming from. Being raised in the public eye, never having the chance to be a child, really caring and loving from the source of his being, I understand that kind of person. They are rare in this world. His lyrics spoke from his soul about so many things. Most of those sincere recordings never got the air time and were never really well known. Most of this type of music never hits the heights of the **Pop Charts**. I'm happy he voiced his concerns about the state of humanity, the state of the Earth and the greed and avarice that rule these days.

This was not the person that the media wanted to be seen, so they created this *"bad guy"* and convinced many that his name was Michael Jackson. When Michael began to get his strength and courage back, and was ready to move ahead and conquer even another generation of adoring child fans he had to be stopped. The media had painted an ugly picture of this man and they wanted to keep him from emerging victorious again. *They found a way to kill him, and to kill his image as well.*

I am not suggesting that Michael, himself, did not play a role in his final demise. I do feel that there were many around him who thought that he was worth a lot more to them dead than he was alive. Besides, they just couldn't allow him to outlive his *"bad boy"* image. That would spoil everything for the **Powers that Rule** in the **Mega-Media Industry**.

I was a personal witness to the death of another great Aboriginal American mega star whose health could have improved with certain natural treatments. Those decision makers around him would not allow the treatments to go forward and the mega star left this world. The star left his riches to those who refused the natural treatments for him.

What is most notable about events since Michael's death is the *emergence of the **Beatles***. I don't know much about the legalities or the ins and outs of the Sony/Jackson ownership of the **Beatles Catalog**, but we sure have seen and heard a lot about them since Jackson's death. **What's up with that?**

From my point of view, Michael was another *Aboriginal American Male Sacrifice.* **His final ten years of life demonstrate that no matter how far an Aboriginal American male climbs up, or how rich he becomes, or how much loved and admired he is, the media, i. e, the "***Powers that Be***, will bring him down. They can not allow a so-called "***black man***" to remain a hero – no matter what. Public disgrace and public execution are the preferred sacrifice. It sells a lot more books, magazines, movie tickets and newspapers. And this is what it's all about. Money!**

It is Difficult to Explain

A few weeks ago a letter from a teenager to B.E.T. (Black Entertainment Network) circulated on the internet. The teenager was outraged over the B.E.T. Awards Ceremony where the sagging pants – necked butt, *boodie* shaking youth were elevated and honored by *"RESPONSIBLE"* adults and hailed as some kind of heroes who deserved recognition.

The teenage girl admonished the adults, including the general public in the Aboriginal American community, for tolerating this type of nonsense, the vile exposure of the rear end of young adult men, the gleeful acceptance of sparsely clad young girls and even the adult women who were B.E.T. presenters. She pointed out how offensive it was to sit in her living room viewing the degradation of Aboriginal women performing for an international audience dressed like pole-dancing strip club performers and grown women looking like prostitutes. Her question was, *"Why is BET allowed to continue to enter our homes glorifying moral deprivation and sexual innuendo?"*

I was so happy to read the teen's letter because while I sat with my adult daughter watching the B.E.T. awards, I had the same question. Why would *"so called"* community leaders such as Al Sharpton and various other famous and responsible adults who spoke or presented awards not say something about those below the butt sagging pants?!? Was everybody too scared or intimidated to comment on the harm that we are doing to our own image world-wide by this kind of overt, sexually explicit abnegation of respect for self and for the women who bore you? Is it more important to look and act like the *"Western culture"* than to show reverence for those who fought and died for our freedom? Has our message simply deteriorated to the level of *"prostitute"* to gain the admiration of those *"powers that be"*? Or have we again become the modern *"Stepping-Fetchit"* of the early days of Hollywood?

I forwarded the young teen's letter to my internet group. I received two responses, one from my warrior Sista, veteran of the Civil Rights Movement and Anti-Apartheid movement and one from my Afro-Swiss Warrior Sista. Warrior Sista from Switzerland wanted to know the owners of B.E.T. I explained that it is now owned by **Viacom**, a super media conglomerate of Euro-Americans. When BET was at its prime under Aboriginal American ownership the Viacom conglomerate gave him a monetary offer that was too good to refuse. With the sale of BET to Viacom all news programming and respectable information entertainment programming was discontinued. What is left now on BET is low budget, low mentality, and bottom of the ghetto *"exploit-tainment"* with little or no morally redemptive substance.

Warrior Woman wanted to know *why the **NAACP** does not complain to **Viacom*** or threaten boycott or sue them for damages to the Aboriginal American image. I told her, **"It's difficult to explain, it's complicated."** But I promised that I would explain when I get the time to write about it.

There is a secretive and insidious, subtle but sinister plot that is at play which has undermined the movement of Aboriginal Americans over the past thirty to forty years. You may say that the threat comes from the *political realm,* **COINTELPRO,** *law*

91

enforcement, the judiciary and the education system. All of this is true, but none of this would be effective if we were in possession of our own minds, our own will! *What do you mean, Mama Kali?*

Well, over the last forty years a war has been waged against the American people from the dinner table and from the water fountain. *What does that mean, Mama Kali?*

Americans have been feed poison from the dinner table and from the water companies in the name of fluoride for **"tooth decay prevention"** in our water and toothpaste and from the artificial sweeteners such as **aspartame**, supposedly used as a low calorie substitute for sugar. Both of *these additives, fluoride and aspartame, are known to work against the autonomous thinking, a strong and independent will, our passion for self-determination and our passion for independent thought and action.*

Over repeated years of exposure through food, water and self-care products our power for independent thoughts and actions weaken, we become docile and malleable like clay, adjusting to the will of *whoever is paying for us to work, dance, sing or to play.* We simply *"go along"* with the will of the master to *"get along"* in the society.

This is all done so that self-determination is no longer a word in our vocabulary. We no longer see ourselves as independent beings with the will or the ability to decide our own destiny. We eat, work, watch TV, sleep, engage in self-indulgent destructive behavior and get sick; then we are handed over to the *"Sick-Care System"*. The balance of our lives are spent taking pharmaceutical drugs. We are at the mercy of the **Sick Care System** to the point where we have no freedom of movement.

Those who are appointed to look after the interests of Aboriginal Americans are also caught in the system. Through their non-profit and religious organizations like the **NAACP, the Urban League, the Rainbow Coalition** and **Faith-Based Church groups**, and untold other organizations supported by *"Foundation Grants"* their income and the power they hold as *"leaders"* and *"spokesperson"* for the down- trodden masses and the *"upper middle class"* income and status makes them *"slaves"* to these organizations. To keep their status they must dance to the tune of the Piper. The Piper is the one behind the poisoning of the food and the water and the *"X-rated black exploitation TV, movies and music"*.

"Oh, Mama Kali, this is just another one of your conspiracy theories!" I hear y'all saying right now. Don't believe me. Go check it out for yourselves. What are the effects of fluoride on human behavior, on mental development, on your health? What is the history of **aspartame** and when did the *"low calorie, no calorie"* craze begin? Why is it that the majority of consumers of *"diet"* sodas are obese and sick?

Of course, fluoride and aspartame are not the only poisons in our food, but they are the major ones that contribute to our docile, disinterested, aloof, uncaring and disengaged, apathetic behavior. We can't fight for ourselves because we don't have the interest or the will to live our lives as independent productive beings. It's just too easy to work for somebody and get paid enough to get along. Why should we bother?!

We are voluntary slaves, house Niggas and field Niggas; some of us are professional slaves in service to the "Massa" – but slaves nonetheless. So what do we do? We stop drinking that water and eating that food. We switch to clean water and clean food. When we can wean ourselves and retrieve our minds we can grab a hold of our own destiny, then we will muster up the nerve to tell our boys to pull up their pants and tell our girls to put on some clothes. These are the first steps to our own redemption.

Mimicking Negative Images

From Western Media

One unfortunate exposure that is having a negative influence in the youth in Ghana, is the "***bad boy, hoodlum, rap videos***" that are shown on TV. Some village boys are wearing their trousers low down over their rear end, exposing their underwear. I am told that the Ghanaian members of parliament are planning to outlaw this type of dress. Sure, freedom of expression is something that we all desire, but to mimic such behavior, which has its roots in the American prison industry, is not only stupid, but it is self-effacing and self destructive. It is my understanding that this style of wearing over-sized low riding trousers came out of the American prison population. Prisoners are given standard sizes and are not allowed to wear a belt. So if the pants are too big, it just rides the rear end. For this style of dress to have infiltrated the Aboriginal American popular culture, and then to move to the African continent, begs for an answer;

"If our role model, idol and aspiration is to become a prisoner, what kind of value system is this?!"

I enjoy the Nigerian produced movies that are shown on television here in Ghana. I like the simplicity of the stories, some which are based on traditional lore and legends. However, I am beginning to see a change in the story lines lately, with the *Hollywood gangster image, and violence toward women mimicked on to*

95

screen.

I was in a department store watching an ongoing video which was playing on simultaneously on several televisions. I was comparing the picture quality, and planning to purchase a TV set. As I gazed at the screens, I realized that something was happening to the woman. There was a man sitting in front of the woman, the woman was moaning and groaning in great pain and agony. The man appeared to be poking something between her legs. I continued to watch the TV screens, amazed that such a scene would be on public display for all to see. Out from between the woman's legs, the man brought a bloody *Coca Cola bottle*! The woman was **being raped with a Coke bottle**!

I was outraged! I asked the sales clerk if he knew the nature of the video that was showing. Did he know what was happening to that woman on the screen? He laughed and ignored me. I asked to see his manager. He pointed to a *suited **East Indian*** near the check out line. I approached the manager and tugged at his arm to follow me. He was shocked that I would touch him, he being the boss and used to the **unspoken caste/class system** in place in most African nations, i.e., white man on top, brown man *(Asians)* in the middle and black man at the bottom. He jerked his arm away from me, but I continued to hold him to the television section of the store. Everyone was amazed that I would take the man by the coat, but as they realized that I was an American, they thought that I just didn't know better.

I told the Indian about the scene in the video, and reprimanded him for allowing such a horrible movie to be in the public view. He blamed the sales clerk saying, *"Oh, these are just Junior Secondary School graduates, they don't have class or sophistication."* **I responded, *"But you hired them and you are responsible!"*** He took the video out of the DVD player and gave it to me. ***"You can have it,"*** he said. I took the DVD, bent it and gave it back to him.

Just a few years ago, a scene like that, a woman being raped, would never be shown on Ghana television, and even though the movie was on a DVD, years ago that level of cruelty and violence against women was not projected in African produced movies. *So the Western influence has penetrated into the culture too much*, and scenes such as this will certainly have an impact on the populous, many who believe that they should imitate everything that they see from Europe and America which shines and glitters.

Many behaviors are created by repeated exposure and circumstances. One major element which contributes greatly to the perpetuation of this belief in European and American superiority is the image of the *"Savior, Jesus Christ"*, as a blond haired, blue eyed man. This image is especially powerful in Africa, because of the ***myth of white supremacy*** and the lack of exposure of the masses of people to the Caucasian race.

In America, because we Aboriginal Americans have so much exposure to Euro-Americans, at work, in school on television, everywhere we look, we see them in all their disguises. Most Africans have never sat down with a European to talk or eat or socialize or exchange ideas in a one-on-one and in an equal setting. Therefore, they do not know the true nature of the European race.

We Aborigines in the Diaspora have a big job, to undo the massive brainwashing that our unsuspecting continental brothers and sisters are subjected to. The belief that all that comes from Europe or America is better than anything in Africa is destructive to all African societies. The images, sights and sounds from the various media sources, especially Hollywood movies, are particularly undermining because they create a desire for material things and encourage negative behaviors to secure these *"things"*. While we are busy buying into the *"shiny"* images and false glamour of the movies, the blue eyed sons and daughters of Europe and America are creeping into these nations, robbing, stealing and cheating their way into *"ownership"* in all industries, including water, electricity, communications, infrastructure and agriculture.

Appraisal of our value systems must be addressed; otherwise we will loose Africa's rich natural resources to the image of the false *"Savior"* and loose our souls to the *"Bling"*.

Attitudes: Are They Transmitted through Genetic Memory?

Today, a young Ghanaian postal worker was upset when I asked her a simple question, *"Why does it take 30 days for a registered letter to be delivered from this post office, when I was told earlier this week at the main post office that delivery will take 7 to 10 days?"*

This question was quite valid to me, since the two post offices were in the same town. But the young girl was annoyed that I had the audacity to question her, so I asked to speak to the postal manager. I had to decide how to post some documents without spending three hundred thousand cedis, which is the monthly salary for many working people in this town.

Based on the answer from the postal manager, I decided to check the speed of the mail and bought a simple stamp, with no frills or registration. I gave the same postal clerk the single bill to pay for the stamp; she picked it up by the edge, as if it was infected with a virus, and dropped it on the counter. I thanked her for being so *"gracious"* and took my letter to the box and posted it.

I have found this attitude to be very common among the working women in the service sector, especially in government offices in Ghana. It is as if they are annoyed that they have to be on the job, and even more annoyed that you want them to perform their job! Then I remembered that this attitude is about the same as that which we see in America, among some American Aboriginal women, especially those in government jobs and the social service

99

sector. They act as if they are doing you a favor to even be there, and if they actually do the job they are paid to do, then you should bow down to them with gratitude and thanks.

One of the best skits that I have seen on *"Saturday Night Live"* comedy show in America was a take off on the American Aboriginal female postal worker. The postal worker had extra long false fingernails painted with extravagant designs, a hairdo that required stiff hair gel; she had an attitude that would make you beat your chest in anger. Whoever wrote that skit certainly had that experience more than one time, because the skit was perfectly written and executed. I laughed until I was in tears.

According to my own experience, not just in the post office, but in many other stores and services, this *"chip on the shoulder, what are you asking me to do"* attitude is prevalent among the African women and the American Aboriginal women. This is certainly not a condemnation of all American Aboriginal women or Ghanaian women, because I have had good service from most. Is it just a coincidence that their expressions, the same smacking of the lips, sucking of the teeth, rolling of the neck, rolling of the eyes are the same in many African countries as well as it is in America? So I wonder if this attitude is transmitted in the D. N. A.

Sometimes I see gestures, posturing and hand waving that look just like the folks standing on the corners in *"the hood"* in America. This tells me for sure that we are cut from a similar cloth . Because we haven't had the exposure to each other's every day life, through media or any other source whereby we can imitate, the idiosyncrasies are too similar, and must *"run in the blood"*.

We really must learn to treat each other better, both on the continent and in the Diaspora. I believe that this lack of respect for our sisters and brothers is simply a lack of respect for ourselves. We cannot make progress if we harbor so much self hatred. I have seen the same workers change their attitude when dealing with people of other races other than our own. No African would dare to display that disrespectful attitude toward a white woman or a white man. They are simply too afraid of Europeans and they revere them. So they grin and shuffle whenever a white person approaches them, the same as many of our people do in the States.

I have witnessed this change of attitude when dealing with the clerks in the local convenience store. The women have always had an attitude here in Ghana, when I visit the store. There have been times when I refused to purchase the products because of their attitudes. It appears as if they don't want to issue a receipt for purchases; the women assume a very nasty posture when I ask for a receipt. One day I refused the purchase because of the poor service. As I was leaving, a European woman was entering the store, so I decided to observe the clerk's behavior. The same clerk, who always treated me like I was dirt, smiled and gave the European woman the most gracious service.

Here is another case in point. There are two wonderful ladies who work at my local post office in South Atlanta, Georgia, USA. Because of my mail order business there, I see these women three to five times a week. They are friendly and helpful, and give me all the respect. One day, however, I arrived at the post office at my usual late hour, near closing time, and one of the ladies told me she was in a very bad mood. I understood, and kept to my business without any small talk. But when the white woman from a local business, whom I always meet at the post office around closing time, arrived a few minutes later, the postal clerk cheerfully greeted her with smiles, laughter and small talk. I made no comment; I simply noted how she changed when she dealt with white people. This behavior is just an example of how we interact with each other, and how we change that behavior when interacting with others whom we either fear or whom we hold in reverence.

Some attitudes, I believe, are a genetic memory. The fun loving, singing and dancing, optimistic, happy and smiling, lively and sociable outlook that we see widespread the African societies, is simply the nature of a people who were blessed by God with abundant food, warm weather and close family ties. Nature did not harm us, but supported us in our natural, easy-living tropical environs. Just as we find Europeans who are cold, unfriendly, selfish, combative, war-mongering and self-absorbed, they are reflective of a hostile environment that demanded that they overpower the elements of the freezing cold weather to survive.

I know that one can not paint everyone with a broad-brush, but there are personality differences that are characteristic of a people. I see it clearly in African societies, just as in the American Aboriginal society. Even though we have been separated for millennia, the genetic memory and behavioral patterns still live, and it is very difficult to erase. Our names have been changed, our language is changed our clothing is changed, our education is changed and our religion is changed, but our behavior has not changed. We are cut from similar cloth. Apparently, it runs in our genes, in our genetic memory.

Let us hold on to the positive traits and nurture them; let us caste out those negative behaviors that keep us angry at each other, and divided us from one another. The strong genetic memory can thrust us forward into a new beginning for the twenty-first century. In the words of the great Osagyefo Dr. Kwame Nkrumah, *"Forward Ever, Backwards – Never!!"*

Battle Scarred and Fatigued

Last night I watched a lecture on DVD, **Warriorhood** [1] given by Mwalimu Baruti. Afterwards I watched a DVD documentary **Yaa Aasantewaa: the Heroism of an African Queen** [2] by Ivor Agyeman-Duah. I was subconsciously preparing for an upcoming battle and I was seeking guidance from somewhere – anywhere, but especially from an Aboriginal perspective.

As an Aboriginal woman surviving with a free mind and spirit after about fifty of my nearly sixty-five years of battle on one front or another, I bear scares on every limb, on every internal organ, especially my heart, my mind and soul and especially my ethereal body, that part of me that is really real and that nobody can see. The looming battle is for my small grandchildren whose quality of life is threatened by a male, the one who is most obligated to protect them.

Brother Baruti used the name *"Asafo"*, an Akan (Ghana) word meaning warrior; an *Asofo* is an action-oriented educator, entrepreneur, and non-intellectual respecter of all people including children, women and elders. An *Asofo* can be a man or a woman. An *Asofo* is also a provider and a protector.

Brother Baruti also talked about *"righteous rage"*, the anger and fury that we Aboriginal people feel and have every right to feel; after all we have been under fierce attack for more than 2,000 years with the last 500 years of captivity and colonization being the most sever and debilitating. Our problem is that our *"righteous rage"* is misdirected, to the people who are closest to us, usually

104

family members and the rage is also deeply internalized to the level of self-destruction and self-undoing.

There are several quotes from **Warriorhood** that I wish to share. I will memorize them and keep them close to my heart as I enter into this battleground.

"He who is ruled by his appetite belongs to the enemy."

> *Ptah-hotep*

"If you are deaf, dumb and blind to what's happening in the world you're under no obligation to do anything. But if you know what is happening and you don't do anything but sit on your ass, then you're nothing but a punk!"

> *Assata Shakur – Aboriginal American Warrior Queen exiled in Cuba*

"A mind attacked and conquered can be easily be guided away from its soul-self."

> *Ayi-Kwei Armah - Two Thousand Seasons*

The documentary about **Queen Mother Yaa Asantewaa** who led the last battle against the onslaught of the British army in 1900 decided to go to war when the men were all ready to give up and surrender to Queen Elizabeth's demand for staggering amounts of gold *and* the *"Golden Stool"*, an Emblem that is the heart and soul of the Asante (Ashanti) Nation. She said these famous words:

"If you men are to behave like cowards you should exchange your loin cloth for my under garments."

She waged the most fierce and bloodiest battle against the British army and was able to escape. She was betrayed by fellow Asantes, and when she was captured and marched away to be exiled to the Seychelles Islands she asked to address her people. She said:

"Women, I weep for you."

One of the men in the gathering then said, *"What about us men?"* The great Queen Mother said,

"What men? The men died on the battlefield!"

So I ask you to pray for me. I am on the way to the battlefield. Perhaps this is my final battle.

Akoben House, www.akobenhouse.com

The Burden

Living in Ghana over the past three years taught me a most valuable lesson, but the words to set the situation onto the radar of realization was while I watched Oprah talk about her weight gain and the reasons for her inability to keep the weight off. While listening and watching her face intently it finally and clearly dawned on me that Aboriginal women carry not only the psychological and emotional weight of their children but also the more burden-ridden weight of the Aboriginal men in their lives. Aboriginal women carry the Aboriginal man's burden.

Daily I watch the African women as they carried their children on their backs along with tremendous weights on their head, balanced perfectly as they walk for long distances in the blazing hot sun and sometimes in the rain. The women in the cities carried the wares they sell in the neighborhoods or in the market places – anything from plantain or smoked fish to fabrics or metal and plastic utility bowls and pots. I have seen items piled up to 3 feet on top of a woman's head; she moved with grace and great skill through the narrow paths or the walkways and stalls of the marketplace. In the villages and countryside the women walked with sticks of firewood five to six feet long, bound by a twine from the bush and piled three feet above their heads; yet they moved effortlessly.

Sometimes men would be walking beside the women – the man carrying a machete in one hand. I seldom saw men accompanying women where the man shared the load or carried the child. The burden was almost never evenly or partially distributed between them. I know that this is a cultural tradition, but to me it seemed that the woman was responsible for too much of the family's basic needs. But this is not a judgment that an outsider can make about a place where I have no real knowledge or long term cultural understanding of. Whenever I made a comment about certain cultural practices, I was met by unwanted looks, comments and even suspicions.

In America and in the Western world Aboriginal women have guarded and protected their men for more than 500 years. Over time the legacy of slavery and the de-humanization and de-de-masculinization of Aboriginal men has escalated in hidden and covert ways and often in ways that the greater society is unaware of. No matter how *accomplished* and *successful* a American Original man becomes in the Western world he is still burdened by an *"inferiority complex"* which is not self imposed but covertly spoken in attitudes and actions of the white society and the *"acceptable"* social order of *"white supremacy"*.

Oprah said that she realized that what she was craving was *"love"* and that she filled the vacuum with food. I sincerely believe that most women crave love and give most of themselves to others
– their children, husbands and families with the resulting self neglect that leads to this *"craving"*.

Loving yourself as a solution to fixing the craving is not the only answer because it is not just lack of love for self but the inability to carry the burden of *"inadequacy"* society imposes on the Aboriginal population and in particular on the Aboriginal man.

But what about Oprah? She's not married and she doesn't have children. What Oprah's personal burden is the social *"child"* that she speaks to daily in her television audience, the *"child"* that is the American society that still behaves like a selfish and self-centered only child. This *"child"* is the unhealed wounds of racism and white supremacy. What Oprah does each day is to rub a little more salve on the *"diabetic wounds"* of the collective soul from the American society. The wound has not and will not heal until the puss and festering disease has been cleansed through open admittance of the presence of the sore and the cleansing of that wound with the application of a healing medicine that can close this open sore on the soul of America.

But this is not the only burden that Oprah carries. I can see it in her eyes whenever I see her with her on-and-off mate, Stedman. I have personally never seen the two of them together – only in pictures. In each of the photos where I have seen them together, I never saw true *"joy"* in their eyes or on their faces. I don't know much about Stedman himself but I do know that Aboriginal men in America and Aboriginal men who interface in the white *"Western"* world show deep gushes on their souls.

Because of the deep love that we original women have for our men, we share the hurt of their deep soul wounds. Because we have carried our men through these hundreds of years of sacrifice so that we can survive as a people, we unwittingly and unknowingly carry this load for them – and it is killing us!

109

As my daughter and I watched Oprah today talking about loving herself and putting herself first and self-care on her daily schedule, I personally wondered how she would deal with the burden that she secretly carries for Stedman? How will she fill that vacuum created by the *"secret burden"* she carries for all Original men? This is a question that I must answer myself, because I know that the weight that I carry is not mine alone, but the weight of the *"wounded soul"* of the men in my life and the collective burden of the Original men whose ultimate realization of *"manhood"* as defined by the Western culture, can not be realized until the wound is carefully cleaned out and a *"healing salve"* has closed the hole in their soul.

All the Aboriginal women that I know carry the weight of the Original man's burden, be it for their father, their brother, their boyfriend or their husband. There is sadness in the eyes that reveals the unspoken truth about that hole in their soul. Even the election of Barack Obama to the Presidency can not heal this *"diabetic wound"* because America continues to apply the latest placating salve and *"masking make-up"* to cover the sore without ever applying the *"healing balm"*.

We, America's original women, to save ourselves we must find a real solution -- a healing solution. It is so clear that stuffing ourselves with food can not mend that hole or relieve the burden. How do we take this on?!? Where do we go fromhere?

In the Absence of a Male Role Model

Just last week I received a long email from another friend in southwestern U.S.; she is a M.D., N.D. and priestess of Oshun. She is having a problem with her high school age son. She is finally divorced, after years of an abusive marriage. Her husband promised to turn all the children against her. The son has no where to go and no one to turn to.

This remains the greatest challenge to our people today. What do we do with our sons? Our sons are products of our own lives; but where did we go wrong? I had a big problem with my oldest daughter when she was a teenager. But she straightened out. Most of the girls do. But our men seem to be lost. What did we do, or didn't do as women, as mothers, as wives?

I know that I can not claim to be anywhere near perfect, and I did all that I thought that a wife and mother should do. In spite of it all, after nearly forty years of service to family, I had to travel 10,000 miles away from my family in order to save myself! I get along with them fine in this far off place; but even with this distance there are challenges.

Much of it has to do with the psychosis that we must develop to live under the apartheid government of America. We tell ourselves all the time that we should stop blaming the white man and look at our own faults. This is like saying that one can live in an ecosystem and not be influenced by it. We all know that

111

our environment plays a major role in our development; hence to say that American apartheid does not influence the outcome of your life is just wishful thinking.

Maybe what we need is a "think tank" of American Indigenous women, real American Indigenous women, and true American Indigenous women. What I mean by this is that we need to form a "think tank" of women who are not in the mold of Condelissa Rice or Baroness Amos (Britain's Condelissa), who are trying hard to be like somebody else. We need a Shirley Chisholm, Sojourner Truth and Fannie Lou Haimer, women who know who they are and will face every danger on the road to liberation. We need to sit down and look at ourselves and decide which direction we want our people to travel. We have no guidelines now, no road map and no parameters. We are just following the lead of "Massa".

It is obvious that those men who are leading us now don't have a clue. Take a look at our US Congressmen and the African Indigenous Presidents. There is only one President that I can feel proud of, that is Mugabe of Zimbabwe. He is the only African Indigenous leader who is not cow-towing to American and European powers. We can not follow these sell-out men or we will meet a certain death, a death of heart, mind and spirit. We are in a comatose state right now!

It is time for the American Indigenous women to step up, step in and take over our future. We have followed the Euro-American-Arabic patriarchal Judaeo-Christian-Islamic model and we see where it has gotten us, i.e., deeper in the cesspool. The model is not working for them either, because if we examine the state of the societies in these nations, they are in as much social turmoil as the American Indigenous societies. The only advantage they have over us is that they are living at a higher level of materialism, but it is the same cesspool.

So I call all real American Indigenous women to the forefront. Let us declare war on the society that is destroying our sons, our men, and let us lead them into another direction. It is the tradition in American Indigenous societies that when things get so terrible, the women call for war. Yes, it will be an arduous and dauntless journey, but what else do we have to do for the rest of our lives? I have nothing else to do but to liberate my grandsons, my grand-daughters and to try to talk to the men. The men can be very stubborn, and sometimes, they fail to act in their own best interest and the interest of the entire family and the entire race!

Can I call a council of grandmothers? Can I call a council of Indigenous women from the continent and throughout the American Indigenous communities, women who are retired, who can take the time to think through a strategy for our liberation? The blueprint has already been thought through by many of our great ones, like Claude Anderson and Amos Wilson. All we have to do is to bring these strategies into the 21st century, put an aboriginal feminine touch to them, attune them to Mother Nature and move! Yes! MOVE!! MOVE!! MOVE!!

Let us plan to come together in Ghana in 2008. Let us plan to meet the Sun at the Summer Solstice in Ghana on June 21, 2008. We have a full year to plan and a full year to save. Let the American Indigenous Female War Babies and Baby Boomers place their mark on this Earth before we rest! After all, it was our generation that caused the change in the 1960's. Apparently, our job is not yet complete. Therefore, let us CHANGE THE WORLD!! CHANGE THE WORLD!! CHANGE THE WORLD!!

We can do it. We have nothing to loose and we have our sons, our men and the whole world to gain. When we traveled to Egypt in 1996, on the way to Ethiopia, where we had been contacted by an Ethiopian mystic, we found the Biblical Manna at Imhotep's pyramid, the Step Pyramid, on the Giza Plateau. Yes, Manna is a real substance, it is not a myth. This is the food that was provided by God to the Children of Israel when they had been lost in the wilderness for 40 years and they believed that all hope was lost. When we found this Manna, we knew that this was a sign from the Most High that, if we as a people move in faith, trusting that the Almighty will always provide for us, we will find success.

The message from the Ethiopian mystic was this.
"Mothers in the Diaspora, Mothers in the Diaspora, who knows what God has for you!"

The message was that the American Indigenous women would lead the world to salvation. Who is better equipped than we are? No one!! NO ONE!!! NO ONE!!!!

Please circulate this letter to all American Indigenous women, real American Indigenous women, who know that at this point, they have nothing to loose. Let us begin to plan our move to join the "think tank" of all American Indigenous Women, especially the Grandmothers, to come together to plan and to implement our plan!! Right Now! RIGHT NOW!! RIGHT NOW!!!

The Call – Answered

The Call was sounded for us to meet for a serious discussion, with resolution and action plans, next year in 2008, in Ghana, West Africa. **The Call** was heard; I have received many emails in response to the **Call.** I know that the time is right, and the **Call** is ripe. We must take hold of the reigns of the horse and lead it to our own salvation. There is no one but us.

It was prophesied from Ethiopia, that we, the Indigenous women, would lead the world to the ultimate salvation. We are the only ones capable at this juncture in the planet's evolution. We have the wisdom and experience, having walked upright for millions of years and having developed the *gluteus maximum* (*rear end muscle*) to the ultimate degree. This muscle is the result of having walked upright for millennium. It is partially the reason why we are still standing. It is difficult to knock us off balance.

Along with our God-given physical strength, it is because of our spiritual development that we have become the sages of the world. We can decide how we will use that sagacity. Will we try to save the whole world at one time, or will we concentrate on saving our own selves first? The flight attendant on the airplane advises you with safety instructions to, in case of trouble, save yourself first, because if you don't place your own oxygen mask on first, you can't save anyone else.

Over the past forty years we have been trying to save other folks, because of our compassion, sympathy, and true humanity. The problem is that, as we were busy throwing out rope to save

115

others, they were busy pulling our children down. We forgot to look behind us, to see what those whom we were attempting to treat fairly, justly, and with kindness, were doing to keep up from surviving and prospering. So, the time has come to concentrate on our own salvation – **FIRST!!!**

For our own preparation, and so that we all have a realistic view of our real psycho-spiritual reality, I share Dr. Amos Wilson's *"The Falsification of African consciousness."* This is **the Bible** explaining *"What Ails Us"* as Aboriginal people. There is no need for us to *"call a Press Conference,"* as Dr. John Henrick Clarke used to accuse us of doing. It is nobody else's business what we are reading or how we plan to survive. We are not taking up any lethal arms; we are only erasing the false information that has been fed to us over hundreds of years.

Our lives, our sagacity will triple, our dignity will rise, and our power will ascend into a crescendo. **Spiritual POWER** is greater than any destructive medium man has made on EARTH, and it belongs to US, the Mothers in the Diaspora. The Powers of the Almighty One are with us. All we need to do is *CALL ON THE POWER, AND IT WILL BE OURS*. We can turn our lives around, the lives of our families and most of all, we can **SAVE OUR OWN – FIRST!!!**I will continue to send support to you all. You can begin by organizing those conscious women in your close circles wherever you are. Don't worry – everyone will not come because many of us are not ready to leave the plantation. That is okay, leave them there. Let the circle reach out, and **LET THE CIRCLE BE UNBROKEN.**

Addiction to Privilege
Admonition from Grandmother
From: Audri Scott-Williams

Our Mother Goddess knew what She was doing when She brought people together in families, clans, communities, villages and then later nations. For progress to move forward it takes more than one person's thoughts, ideas, visions, plans and initiatives. When I received the timely email from our Sista, Audi Scott-Williams, who has been on an around-the-world walk for peace since 2005, she sparked a realization in me which addresses a serious condition in the African Diaspora (American Aborigine) communities in North America.   That condition is an addiction to privilege. It is short-cut way of saying that we are spoiled by the advantages and comforts of living in a rich, developed nation where all the comforts of the modern world are at our disposal – as long as you *"trust and obey"* the white man and don't *"rock the boat."*

Even though Aborigine Scholars talk about and write about *White Privilege* we seldom acknowledge or even consider that by virtue of living in these countries we also enjoy a level of comfort and privilege that most of the peoples of the world have little or no access to. On a broad basis, Africans (Aborigines) in America enjoy private cars, spacious living quarters, electricity, refrigerators, running water, flushing toilets and for many central heat and/or air conditioning. In Ghana where I have lived for the last 19 months the majority of the people do not have access to most of these conveniences. Just having electricity and a refrigerator are considered an accomplishment for many.

Even though we who live in the western societies know that these conveniences are commonplace and considered a necessity, it is still more than what most people in this world have. Hence, I understand the reality that Grandmother Audi Scott-Williams is reminding us of. Our unwillingness to change our level of comfort on this earth has made us subjects *captive chattel* in the western world. This is reminiscent of the Biblical quote from **Exodus,** when Moses was leading the people out of slavery, and they complained to him and Aaron that they must have been crazy to follow him out of their comfort zone where they were *chattel, in service to the Pharaoh.*

> **And the whole congregation of children of Israel grumbled against Moses and Aaron in the wilderness..And the children of Israel said unto them:**
>
> *"Would to God we had died by the hand of the Lord*
> *in the land of Egypt, when we sat by the flesh pots,*
> *and when we did eat bread to the full; for ye have*
> *brought us forth into this wilderness, to kill this whole assembly with hunger."*
>
> **Then the Lord said unto Moses,**
> *"Behold, I will rain bread from heavenfor you,*
> *and the people shall go out and gather a*
> *certain rate every day, that I may prove them,*
> *whether they will walk in my law, or no."*

And when the dew that lay was gone up, behold, upon the face of the wilderness there lay a small round thing, as small as the hoar frost on the ground. And when the children of Israel saw it, they said one to another,
> *It is the Manna."*

> **And Moses said unto them**
> *"This is the bread which the Lord hath given you to eat."*
> **Exodus 16: 2…3…4…14…15**

When my partner and I were on our way to Ethiopia to see the **Ethiopian Prophet** who summoned us to give us the prophesy about the women of the African (Aboriginal) Diaspora leading our people out of bondage in the *New* (western) *world*, we stopped at **Imhotep's Step Pyramid at Sankara on the Giza Plateau in Egypt. It was there that we found the *Manna* of the Bible.** From that day forward, I knew that the Ethiopian prophesy was real and that I, Mama Kali, was now obligated to tell our people that we must take that bold step to move away from the *"flesh pots and bread"* of the western world. We must consider travel away from the stolen land to find our own home, to find our own identity and to acknowledge the ancestors.

Are we bold enough and brave enough to move away from what we perceive to be *"privilege"* in America? Are all of these things a *"privilege?"* Are we so addicted to the food and the creature comforts that we are willing to watch our children and grandchildren being sold away into the **Prison Industry**? Can we not give up just a small amount of comfort to salvage our own self-respect and sense of dignity? Or are the pizza and hamburgers, the colas and chitterlings (*chitlins*) so sumptuous that we will die to keep the grease falling from our lips? Can we muster up the courage of Grandmother Audri and find an alternative destiny for our own flesh and blood?

I think that we can; it requires that we wean ourselves… little by little. Let us start by reducing the excesses of American holidays like Halloween, Thanksgiving and XMAS. All of us know that we don't need any of these things to find peace, harmony and salvation for ourselves and our FUTURE!!! Why do we trouble ourselves with the consequences? Let us not be **coerced, seduced and maligned by** *"Powers of Darkness"* **to work against our own best interest. Let us not be seduced by the lure of advertising of things that we don't need and usually don't really want.** Let us go *"Back to the Future"* to find our true selves and to create a much better **TOMORROW**.

"Courage is not the lack of fear but the ability to carry on in spite of it." Author Unknown Africa; October 14, 2007

Grandmothers in Ghana – Purpose

The 1ˢᵗ Annual Organizing Think Tank

To establish a Place of Respite and Solace for Mature Women & Men in the Aboriginal Diaspora to Re-Train Our Grandchildren – Our Future

TO: Create an Environment for Growth, Learning & Conscious Development of the Mind, Body and Spirit in the Ways of our Ancient Ancestors

Provide an Alternative Reality, a Different Living Space for our Children who are Lost in the Westernized System aimed at their Self-destruction & Self-undoing

Raise the level of Consciousness, Possibilities and Spiritual Enlightenment for Adults & Children using Mother Nature's Infinite & Abundant Resources for Natural Living

Where:Elmina – Cape Coast Central Region of Ghana, West Africa

When: June 24 – July 9, 2008; Four Day Intensive -- June 30-July 3, 2008

Who: North Scale Education & Research Institute, College
                Park,GA Elmina, Ghana (Mama Kali Sichen)
The G.E.N.E.S.I.S. Project (*Growing Energy &*
Nutrition for Environmental Stability & Investments in our Societies)

How: 1. Register for Four Day Intensive

120

2. Meet & Greet Chiefs & Village Elders

3. Planning the Kibbutz-like Training Facility for our Children from the Afrikan Diaspora in Need of Reorganizing their Lives & their Thinking

4. Organizing Volunteers from the Afrikan Diaspora to Operate Training Facility for our Children/Grandchildren

5. Curriculum Planning in the Ancient Ways ~ The Seven Liberal Arts, the Ten Virtues & the Forty-two Principles of Ma-at (7.10.42)

6. Introduction to the Basic Sciences of Agriculture/Horticulture, Survival a Self-sufficiency

Contact Us: North Scale Institute, 5580 Feldwood Pl, College Park, GA 30349

Phone: 404 767-4786

The G.E.N.E.S.I.S. Project, Cape Coast, Ghana

G.E.N.E.S.I.S. Projects also in Anomabo, Nsanfo & Elmina, Ghana

**Grandmothers at a fashion show and musical event,
Cape Coast.**

Grandmothers in Ghana at beach resort, Elmina.

Tony peeks from behind Mama Kali at Elmina Castle Restaurant. He traveled from America with his grandmother to the Grandmothers Conference in Ghana.

Underground Boycott

Like the underground railroad of yesteryear today on October 2, 2007 we must be mindful that if our plans for a national boycott are to succeed we must move quietly on this issue. Why? Because the agents of white supremacy who live among us, who have for too long unfairly influenced our lives, will intervene on behalf of their bosses, the white elite ruling body of America, to confuse us and lull us back into the complacency of *"going along to get along"*.

We all know who these people are, the Negro Disciples of White Supremacy. They are called *"Black leaders"*. They are summoned as spokespersons whenever anything happens to warrant comment in our communities. They are appointed and paid for by the bosses, either through non-profit companies, organizations or churches. One of the latest payoffs was to the preachers in the *"faith-based-initiative"*. When the pastor accepted the money for the child day care or elders' day care facility, he/she also signed on as a supporter of the "powers-that-be". If he dares to drift from his/her appointed agenda for control of our communities, not only will he be publicly dishonored, humiliated and emasculated, he will also be imprisoned on *"trumped-up charges"*, usually called *"misappropriation of funds"*.

Therefore, we must move with caution and care to continue with the national-international boycott of *"Halloween"* (a celebration of evil demons), thanksgiving (a celebration of the genocide of the copper colored/red people of America, i.e. us), and Xmas (a last gasp grab for your money by people who don't believe in Christ (bankers/Jews) and who don't celebrate Xmas (Chinese-Japanese-Korean toy-gadget makers).

There is no need to call a press conference, as our esteemed Elder, Dr. John Henrik Clarke cautioned us. There is no need to inform the people at work who will go to tell your boss what you are doing. All we have to do is to keep our purse closed, and to buy only books and educational materials for our children and grandchildren from our own bookstores, and online suppliers. We have to learn to say **"NO"** to every little whim, wish, fancy and advertising gimmick that is thrown to our children and grandchildren through the media. Our children and grandchildren will survive.

Whisper in the ears of your *"conscious friends, relatives and co-workers"* about our plan to boycott these holidays. Encourage them to join us in a crusade to liberate our selves and our children from the clasp of white supremacy and misguided materialism, what is in reality – Neo-slavery.

On these holidays, because people will have the day off (usually) you can enjoy family walks in the park, a day at the local greenhouse (in cold places), a day at the riverside of beachfront (in warmer areas), and just some time sitting and talking with family, friends and neighbors. Save your money to bring you to Ghana in 2008!

Our Children Everywhere

I have been following the Jena 6 story through the internet. I heard a 30 second bite on Ghana TV about the protest march, but the way that it was reported the report did not give any explanation of what was happening; so no one in Ghana except for African Americans really understand what is happening. What is happening to Alabama kids is the same that is happening to all our children everywhere.

This is why we must gather together as a think tank to address and resolve these problems with alternative solutions. We can no longer continue to do the same things in the same ways and expect different results. Behavior of this nature is called "*insanity*." We must look for different solutions. I have some definite ideas about alternative realities to place our children into. We need to come together to give birth to these ideas.

Mimi with Esi, Sofi, and Kofi on Moringa Farm.

Anomabo Welcomes You

I traveled to Anomabo yesterday to see Auntie Matilda. She had arranged a meeting with the Paramount Chief, Nana Ammomu about land for farming, and about plans to develop an energy drink with a fruit base from the locally grown fruits. They are pointing me in a direction about 4 miles inland from the coast, which sounds really good, because that would only be about 30 minutes from Elmina. They will show me several available lands for me to do the preliminary selection; when you arrive we can see the ones that are most suitable for the Moringa growing.

The Chief appeared to be a very nice man, who was very interested in having someone come to bring new products and new activity to his district. Nana Ammomu has 64 villages under him, and they reach far into the interior, very close into the rain forest region. He says that there are too many citrus groves with fruits going to waste, and he would be grateful if we took up the chore of reviving this industry. A citrus growers' cooperative is what might work well, with the right minded people working and right hearted people managing, this could work well for everyone.

I also talked on the telephone to the development Chief, who was then in Accra. He is presently importing an energy drink from Germany, which he advertises heavily on TV. He says that he is interested in promoting such a drink made in Ghana, especially if it benefits the agriculture and manufacturing in his district. So I will meet with him, the Paramount Chief and Auntie Matilda one day next week.

Because our next product will be an energy drink with a Moringa base, it would be in our interest to fully utilize the source of the fruit drink. The flash-freezing process which Chuck Banks mentioned sounds like just the way we could process the fresh juice here and manufacture in the US, or even better, to manufacture here and export the bulk to the US in a frozen form, to be thawed and bottled in the US. All of this depends on how easy it will be to import the semi-processed food item. This would be determined by cost effectiveness, etc.

I am especially happy to meet Auntie Matilda. She will be 70 years old her next birthday, and she is a real champion, a strong business woman, self assured and determined. With her guidance through the different roadways, I'm certain that we will have an easier way toward developing the industry, both manufacturing and farming.

This is really what G.E.N.E.S.I.S. is about, using the natural resources to create wealth and prosperity for all. If there are any questions, give me a call.

Greetings from the Eastern Shore of the Atlantic Ocean

The Almighty One has filled my life with so many chores and blessings that I barely have time for rest. Today is a down day, and I have spent a good part of the day resting on my bed. I caught a slight cold, with this winter Harmattan, the blowing sands of the Sahara Desert which descend upon West Africa. It leaves a red haze in the sky along with cool nights, and some cool days. Today is windy but a little hot.

Along with my duties of building up the Nebedaye-Moringa farm, and to oversee the construction of our clinic/healing center here in Elmina, I have taken on a village project at Iture, a G.E.N.E.S.I.S. Youth Initiative. It is difficult to get people started in self-help, as we know all too well among the Aboriginal Americans. Everyone wants the benefits of clean-up and beautification, but very few people are willing to do the work to make these things happen. I am one of those rare people who must stay busy doing something constructive. I have to see progress at the end of the day. I would not succeed as an "idle rich". I would be ousted from the club.

No worry about me becoming an "idle rich" because there are too many people who can benefit from so little, and my personal needs are small. Hence, I could never live an all consuming and self-indulgent life. I give thanks for small needs. I need your help to kick start the G.E.N.E.S.I.S. Project here in Iture. Please send me one dollar or five dollars in an envelope. It will go a long way. I know that when one asks for many dollars, seldom do we receive it. But one dollar is small enough so that you will not miss it. Add a sixty cent stamp and send it on the way.

Kali Sichen, Project Director
THE GENESIS PROJECT
P. O. Box EL 131
Elmina, Ghana, West Africa

Any amount is appreciated. If you send $20.00 you will receive the new G.E.N.E.S.I.S. T-shirt. It is a bright yellow T-shirt with palm-green logo and lettering; it has the G.E.N.E..S.I.S. Logo and it boasts of our G.E.N.E.S.I.S. works in Atlanta, Elmina and Anomabo, where the farm is located.

Best Wishes for You & Yours for this New Year. May the Almighty One Protect You and Keep You Safe.

Mama Kali from Iture, Elmina Ghana

P. S. Several people sent me small money in envelops, I am told; I never received any of these. Therefore, it is not a good idea to send a few dollars in an envelop. It is just too tempting to the postal workers.

Escaping the United Den of Snakes

March 22, 2008

A snake pit is no fun in the winter time. Everyone is locked up inside a closed area without fresh circulating air. Everything is too close and there is no place for mental clarity or to cultivate a clear aura. Therefore, the overlaps of energies, breaths, viruses, bacteria and whatever other entities attach to your person when you move into and out of confined spaces, either public or private, tend to cling to everything you touch.

I was happy to return to Ghana in one piece, although pieces of me are still straggling in from across the water. I vowed never to go to America in the winter time again, especially to any cold places. My body has adjusted to the airy warmth of tropical Africa and there is no good reason for me to force a change into the negative and icy conditions of winter *"wonderlands"*. The *"wonder" is how did you ever survive?*

I have not yet reached my home in Elmina; after six days in Ghana, I have only reached Cape Coast. I brought along a very bad cold and a cough. The warm sun and the clear breeze are shunning the cold away from my chest. I will go to my own home on Tuesday after the long Easter holiday that everyone takes here in Ghana, from Good Friday through Easter Monday. When I was a little girl there used to be a long Easter holiday celebration in North Carolina where I was born. My mother and all our neighbors never planted their gardens until *AFTER* Easter. Now I know why, astrologically, because the Sun (masculine energy) and Moon (feminine energy) make their first encounter after the Spring Equinox (equal day and nights). Most Americans no longer care about these holidays and there is no time off from work.

Yes, I am back in Ghana and my Spirit is slowly beginning to unwind. I don't want to go into any long treatise about how hard it is to extricate myself from the hissing snakes attempting to attach themselves to every arm, leg, breath and word of my being. I am only happy to say that I escaped – and now I can get back to being human and to continue my work to pull the women in the African and Aboriginal Diaspora together, as many as can hear over the loud hissing in the snake pit – and I will begin to summon them into a more compatible realm.

Religious Dogma and the Enslaved Mind

During the Festival weekend I visited friends and their family elders. We gathered for a brief visit in the ancestral home town. Our plan was to join the rest of the family the next day in their parents' ancestral village, a small town to the southeast.

I caught a cold after washing my hair and sleeping under an air conditioner the night before we traveled. Then we drove many miles with the car air conditioner on my face. I was sick and in no condition to travel further. I stayed with an elderly female friend.

It was Sunday morning. The elder told me that she was about to listen to a religious broadcast in her bedroom. She spoke so highly of the preacher that I told her that I would also listen. She joined me in the family meeting hall.

CNN was on when I entered the room and the breaking news was that the former Mayor of Washington DC had been arrested for stalking a woman. I wondered if Marion Barry had been set up again, whether there is something happening in DC whereby they don't want his knowing eyes to glean, or whether he was just living below the belly button.

My elder entered the hall and I quickly tuned to the religious channel. The first thing that I noticed on that channel, was that the program started out with a high-pitched selling spree; books, CDs and online prayer services. Afterwards I noticed that, instead of a crucifix or a stained glass window behind the choir and preacher podium, there was the *"all seeing eye"* very similar to the eye over the pyramid on the dollar bill. I gleaned a connection between the sales pitch and the symbol of the *"all seeing eye"* above the preacher's head.

The message had a very significant meaning. The preacher spoke about how adversity creates character and that the adversities that we experience in our lives are really our blessings. I agreed with him on this issue. I know that the obstacle placed in my path as I have grown have made me a stronger person. The preacher further related

Paul's trials in Rome as the adversities that allowed him to spread the gospel while he was imprisoned. He related the events of Paul's imprisonment (*he stated that he researched this aspect*) whereby Paul was chained to the prison guards in 6 hour shifts. As a result he was able to preach the gospel to four individuals on a daily basis (*I don't know when he slept*).

After the sermon, and many other sales pitches, the elder and I sat down at the kitchen table for a cup of tea. Another preacher was on TV with a different style and a different audience – the Black church style. The elder commented that she didn't like this kind of preaching because she didn't believe that all the shouting and "*Amen's*" and "*Hallelujahs*" were necessary and certainly did not teach anything.

I reminded the elder of the sermon we had just heard, where the other preacher had said that those soldiers to whom Paul was chained and to whom he preached the gospel, they moved forth into Rome to preach the gospel in their own way. "***Sometimes the soldiers preached for their own benefit and their own self-aggrandizement,***" the former, all seeing eye preacher, had just announced. He said that this was okay
– that as long as the word was being preached it did not matter how the word got out or by whom the word was delivered.

Well, why did I use the "***good preacher's***" words to justify the "***bad preacher's***" style of preaching to the elder? She attacked me with a ferocity that frightened me! It was if she had been waiting for the chance to put me down! These were the declarations, pronouncements, assertions, allegations leveled at me:

You can't question the Bible. It is the word of God! God wrote the Bible.

There is no book that pre-date the Bible and how could I say that the Bible came from older and more ancient texts

You are a sinner if you have not been saved. Jesus died on the cross to forgive our sins.

We were all born in sin and could only be saved if we accepted Jesus as our only salvation.

Jesus and God are the same. Jesus did not say that *"your body is a temple of the almighty God."* Jesus only meant that he is God

No matter what other religion you believe in, if you don't believe in Jesus you can not go to heaven

Even in your daily works, if you save the lives of 10 million people you will not be saved unless you accept Jesus as your Lord and Savior.

Never mind any great spiritual leader of any other religion, if he was not saved by Jesus he will never enter heaven.

The Jewish can not be saved because they don't believe in Jesus.

All the work that they on this earth will mean nothing because they don't believe in Jesus.

After this exchange I thought it best not to say anything more to my elder. I turned my attention to the rain and said that I hope that there is no delay in my return home to my village. The elder woman and I spent a few uneasy moments together as I waited for a car to arrive to return to my village.

Personally, I see very little difference in religious zealots, whether they are Christians who adamantly declare everybody a sin-ner except those who have been *"saved"*, or whether they strap dynamite around their bodies to be martyred with the expectation of entering heaven to be rewarded with their own 17 personal virgins (*as promised by many Islamic fundamentalist sects*). Each of these religious zealots is standing as judge and jury in condemnation of another person's life.

137

I believe that anyone who lives a righteous life as laid out by the **10 Commandments** in the Christian Bible or the **42 Principles of Ma-at**, the ancient Egyptian Principles of Righteous Living from which the 10 Commandments evolved, has justified their existence on earth and paid their dues to humanity and to the Almighty Great Spirit. Don't forget the *Moses was raised in the House of the Pharaohs and was educated in the Egyptian Mystery Schools.* Hence when he took the 10 Commandments to the Hebrews he simply taught them what he had been taught by the Egyptians. He modified those principles down from 42 to 10 very likely perhaps many of the Hebrews were not learned enough to understand the sophistication of some of 42 Principle of Ma- at.

I write about this because I am so very hurt that *there are so many people with such small minds that they can not grasp the bigness, the immensity of God-- the Great Spirit. God the Omnipotent, Omnipresent, Omniscient can not harbor ill against good deeds on earth,* no matter who that Good Samaritan is or how they choose to worship. I believe in God with all my heart, all my soul and all my might. I know that when I walk with good intentions and good deeds, *Great Spirit* walks with me. I know that my intentions for good do not go unrecognized. Good intentions can not be ignored by an all seeing, all gracious, all benevolent God. God is not so small that only Christians can be saved. God would not curse 80% of the world's population because they don't believe in Jesus. *God is not and can not be that small.*

God does not ask us to justify our existence through the *"blood of Jesus"*. God has not set us to be judged by those who claimed to be *"saved"*. My question is this – Who decides that one has been *"saved"*? Has God appointed someone on earth who decides who is *"saved"*? Or is this salvation decided by an announcement from the person who claims to be *"saved"*. Who do you trust?

My personal bond is with the Almighty Great Spirit and it needs no justification or recognition from any earthly being.

This is the wave of the Spiritual Transition that is moving across this planet. The Age of Aquarius, the Age of Man's Spiritual Evolution into Christ-Consciousness has begun. There are those of us who are ready will ride that first wave into personal peace, prosperity and freedom. Those who cling to the remnants of the Piscean Age may be overlooked because of their mental enslavement by religious dogma.

Religious zealots peculiar to the religions of the last 2,000 years may find themselves without a boat when the Great Tsunami of Spiritual Enlightenment sweeps across this Brave New World.

African Belief in White Supremacy
To Carol in Switzerland

Don't fret, don't despair that the Africans in your European town have no interest in the true history of Christianity and Judaism. The problem is that an overwhelming number of Africans from the continent don't believe they have any self-worth or value. This is a fact. I have lived and worked side-by-side with many of them on the continent for three years. The white Christ is so embedded in their psyche that nothing at all can erase this image – nothing at all. Many Africans on the continent believe in white man more than white man believes in himself. So many Continental Africans believe that the real heaven is in Europe and America, and if they can only get there they will surely serve white man and make him proud of them and perhaps even "**ACCEPT**" them!

What I am saying is absolute fact. Many on the continent don't even believe their own African brothers and sisters who tell them the truth about Christianity and Judaism. I believe that white Jews brought the Ethiopians to Israel and to America (there are tens of thousands of them in America) to dissuade them from following their own authentic religions. If the Europeans can convince the Ethiopians to abandon their Indigenous Hebrew/Coptic faith, the only true vestiges of authentic Judaeo/Christian worship, then Ethiopians will soon forget and begin to follow the false gods of the whites.

Go right ahead and bring together those few Afro-Europeans who are willing to listen. Let the Diaspora Africans of mixed race hear the truth, because they are more likely to benefit. Like Aboriginal Americans, they do not fall down and worship Europeans because those of us who have lived with them all our lives have seen their naked behinds and we know there is nothing there.

Plan another venue far out into the future. I have been thinking about ways to bring a group of Aboriginal women to Europe for the Black Madonna tour. I'm sure that the group would be so pleased to hear your research as well. Don't despair, my friend. I can tell you that I have talked about how bad the American diet has been for the past 35 years, and only recently have the ordinary people begun to talk about it. Truth takes a long time to be heard.

Totting Christianity to Africa
Diaspora Americans Don the
Cloak of Missionary

I escaped the America in search of peace, quiet and comfort. The stresses of the *"civilized world"* had taken its toll on me. To save myself, I traveled a tiny fishing village on the Coast of Ghana; it was a fitting retreat to secure a bit of solace from a demanding business and a demanding relationship.

Mother Luck found me a comfortable place to live, with a mature woman from New York, who had made a place of retreat for her children and friends, comfort in what we believed to be our Mother Land. As Luck would have it, I asked if there was possibly a permanent place to lay my head, and within a day, I was introduced to a local man who domiciled in France. He had built a vacation cottage on the ocean front. He was returning to France in a few days, and was looking to lease his cottage for two years.

As Destiny would dictate as well, the cottage was beside a church pastured by European American Christian Missionaries, who had raised a family in Africa. However, the family no longer lived at the Mission. Rumor had it that they were run out of town when they ventured into a remote village with the message that those villages didn't want to hear.

That wasn't the end of my confrontation with the Christian dogma. As a child of 12 years, I rejected Christianity when I discovered the hypocrisy of the church elders and community leaders in the southern town where I grew up. To further complicate my own beliefs and values, I received messages to expect family friends in Elmina, who were passing through on tour. Ironically, both of the friends were women, and both were Christian ministers.

This posed a dilemma for me. Both of the women I knew and loved; they both were really good people. They were sincere, good hearted and out to make a difference in the lives of the people they met. These women were not at all in the category of the pedophile priests who disgraced Catholicism, the television preaching warmongering hypocrites who blemished the face of evangelism and the Baptist ministers who don't know how to keep their pants up and their hands out of their parishioners' pockets.

These two women were matured women who had worked hard all their lives, had raised wonderful children and still had more time and more heart to give in service to others. So I thought to myself, how do I handle this situation, with people I deeply respect and admire, who were totting a philosophy that I question? Then I asked, why are they totting this philosophy?

It has been extremely difficult to teach the truth about anything in America. Americans have been hoodwinked into thinking that they live in a country of freedom of information, freedom of the press and freedom of expression. What the majority of the people do not understand is that none of this is true. Revelations over the past months have uncovered a leadership, presidential and congressional, whose greatest efforts are designed to keep the public from knowing the truth about anything. All forms of media, including radio, television, newspapers and magazines all belong to a few wealthy families, and only the news that serves their interest in published.

Educational institutions do an even greater disservice in teaching truth, especially about the history of this world. As a result, the Christian dogma, which sanctioned the genocide of Aboriginal-Indigenous Americans, the robbery of their land, the enslavement of these Indigenous Indians, for the wealth and financial gain of the ruling class, has left out the truth about these evil deeds from the books used for education and learning. They have instead justified their evil deed in the name of teaching *"Christian values"* and *"salvation through Christ"*.

What I can't understand is how anyone, especially intelligent, educated thinkers, can not see that those who are bringing the teachings of Christ are doing the greatest evil in this world, in the name of Christ. Why can't these women, whom I respect and appreciate so much, see that the greatest enemy to the well being of the African people, to whom they are preaching the word of Christ, is the Church elders, the messenger whose word they preach?

When I listen to *"Christians"* speak of their *"salvation"*, I believe that they leave their thinking brains on the bed pillows when they go to church. Logic would ask questions, especially in Africa, how has Christ saved them when they sit at the entry to a gold mine in their own land, and beg for food? Why is it that the wealth, by which the entire world sets a standard value, gold, is found mostly in the land where the poorest people live? If Christ is your salvation, why are you suffering from a lack of basic survival goods and services?

Then my question to the Diaspora African missionaries is this – *"How can you support a doctrine that denies the basic survival goods and human rights to the people to whom you minister?"* In the case of my two women ministers, I know that they both are aware that the wealth of the European and American people comes out of Africa. If the natural resources of Africa were to cease shipping tomorrow, every assembly line, every production facility, every stock market in the world would collapse within 24 hours, and the world's economy would crash within three days.

So what do the African people get for holding the world on their shoulders? They get *"salvation through the blood of Christ"*. They don't get enough food, clothing, health care, clean water, roads, decent housing or education for their children– any of these! They just get *"salvation"*.

Frankly, I wish I knew what *"salvation"* means!! If salvation means to *"save"*, then how are they being *"saved"*, and what are they being *"saved"* from? Salvation can mean *"deliverance"*; are the Africans being delivered from poverty, hunger, poor health care? Salvation can mean *"rescue"*; are the Africans being rescued from hopelessness, exploitation or malnutrition? Salvation can mean *"recovery"*; are the Africans recovering their stolen land, their stolen resources and their stolen people?

Most interesting of all is that *"deliverance"* can mean *"escape"*. This, I believe, is the true meaning of *"salvation through the blood of Christ"*. Salvation, as it applies to the Christian doctrine serving the African people, is that they are provided an *"escape"* from the truth of their lives. Instead of food they are feed rhetoric, instead of water they drink Christian gospel songs which don't even apply to them; i.e., *"Amazing grace, how sweet the sound, to save a wretch like me"*. This song was written by a slave trader who knew that trafficking in human beings was a wretched business, hence, he was the *"wretch"* who was grateful to be saved. This song doesn't apply to the African.

Another song, *"I will cling to the old rugged cross, and exchange it someday for a crown"*. Africans were wearing crowns when they were given Christianity, and in exchange for the crowns, their Kings were given the title of *"chief"*, which stripped them of their royal titles. Instead of wearing their own traditional clothing today, their meager salaries only allow them to purchase those discarded, used clothing of their European and American exploiters.

This one day allowed for *"escape"* from your earthly burdens, to seek *"salvation"* in a promised afterlife, keeps the African in tow, so that their Euro-American exploiters can continue to enjoy this life in the *"here and now"*. If all who use these words would simply take your brains with you to church next Sunday, and ask questions about the sermon you are being *"spoon-fed"*, you would leave the church with clarity and focus, instead of more sand in your eyes.

The masses have been mesmerized, put to sleep, and zombie-fied, walking around in a deep sleep, under the spell of an evil demon, in the guise of Christian church elders. The preachers and elders have convinced the people, in spite of all logical evidence, that he is their salvation.

It is the lack of education about self and your history, which has placed all the people in this stupor. You cannot operate in darkness, and it is the darkness of ignorance and knowledge of yourself and your history, that allows for the evil demon to possess you!

Both of the women ministers are well educated. In fact, one who just graduated from Divinity school was traveling with her professor on a group tour of Africa. Hence, you must question the type of education they received. Were they given the true history of Christianity? Do they know about the original battle that loomed over Christianity from its inception in Africa until the days of **Constantine** and the *Council of Nicaea in 425 AD*? Do they know about Constantine's ongoing dispute with the African Elders of the Church, and Arius in particular? Do they know the role of the Roman Ptolemy family and Serapes, who wanted to introduce himself and the Romans as *"gods"* into the hierarchy of the saints? Do they know about the oldest church in Europe, built by Africans in Constantinople, in honor of the Mother-Goddess/Wisdom, the Hygia Sophia? Do they know that the first popes of the Church, which was the Coptic Egyptian Christian church, were Africans? Do they know about the paintings of Michelangelo and the depiction of Jesus as a blonde-haired, blue-eyed man?

Do they know how women were removed from the Holy Trinity at the inception of the patriarchal dominance of the Church, i.e the Father, Son & Holy Ghost instead of the Father, Mother and Son? Do they know that the original Madonna and Child were not Mary and Jesus but Isis (Auset) and Horus (Heru), the Black Madonna who is still worshiped in Europe, and the Vatican instead of the white Mary and Jesus? Can women go forward into a church that denies them their just place in the hierarchy and the scriptures?

If these teachings were not a part of the learning of the Christian missionaries, then they have not been given the truth in the so-called *"truths"* that they preach. As a result, they are totting the deceptions and lies of enslavement and *indoctrination to Africa for the "slave*

146

master" himself. No longer does the European or American missionary have to endanger his own life in the tropical heat, risking malaria and other tropical diseases. He has sufficiently trained his *"servants"* in the African and Aboriginal Diaspora to act on his behalf, to assure his dominance and white supremacy for at least another generation.

I do not blame these wonderful women whose hearts and souls are given to their work. They are victims of a cruel demon who purports to be godly. If the *"devil"* lives among us, who is credited with the *"sins"* that we are to be *"saved"* from really exists, and if he possesses all this power, don't we realize that he would disguise himself as a saint to lure us into his unsuspecting trap? Certainly he would point to someone else as the *"evil one"* as is the case today, with Christianity and Judaism pointing to Islam as the *"demon"* and Islam pointing to Christianity and Judaism as the *"demon"*. Critical analysis is needed by thinking persons to examine these *"isms"* for themselves, in order to free themselves from religious dogma and **"false prophets"**.

As for the *"gifts"* the African Diaspora missionaries bring to Africa, I have heard many church preachers and elders brag about the churches, clinics and schools their American parishioners are building in Africa. Clinics and schools are desperately needed, provided they are not a continuation of the religious dogma and indoctrination processes. I believe that these congregations would better serve these African communities by digging wells for fresh, clean water, providing sanitation in the form of toilets and bathing facilities and assisting with irrigation in dry places so that the people would thrive in a truly *"clean and godly"* environment. Sanitation is far more needed in Africa than any church building, and if each congregation in the African Diaspora provides one village with just these facilities, that congregation has really acted in the true sense of Christian salvation.

I know that by writing these words and asking these questions, I will be called all kinds of names, *"savage, heathen, demon, and devil worshipper, blasphemous"* and a multitude of words more damaging. But I quote a friend and elder, **"Condemnation without investigation is the height of ignorance."**

In concluding, I beg you to please investigate these religious teachings before repeating words you don't understand and ***"totting indoctrination and mental enslavement"*** to people you think you are *"saving"*!! Investigate, read your history, ask questions at the theology schools, ask questions of your minister. If they are unable to give you sensible and concise answers, you are being misled and mis-educated.

> Accept nothing on blind faith! Don't be led to **"gas chambers"** on blind faith! Don't feed your children (***your future***) or your parishioners a *" faith"* just because you were fed that same *" faith"*.

"Faith pills" do not always cure us from disease; sometimes

they kill us!

Children at beach in their Ghana after 50 years celebration clothing.

Ghana After 50 Years - Part I
King Leopold 98% ~ Kwame Nkrumah 2%

We approach the 50th Anniversary of Ghana's Independence from colonial rule. On March 7, 2007 the battle for the hearts and minds of the Ghanaian people is almost over, and King Leopold Mandate[1] of 1883 is almost exacted and irreversible. In a nutshell, King Leopold of Belgium mandated that the colonial missionaries carry out the following: (1) to bring the Christian message of European Superiority based on the white Christ being the *"Savior"* of African people, and that the missionaries were the right hand of God; (2) Africans should love only European values and heroes and disdain anything from their ancestors; (3) Africans should *"trust and obey"* the missionaries over and above the rules and sanction of parental or indigenous rulers; (4) Africans should love poverty and never question the value of anything in their own homeland, especially the mineral wealth below the soil; (5) missionaries should teach the Africans to *"read but not to reason"*. (6) through church confession, the missionaries should get them to reveal all dissenters, and finally, (7) to target the young.

This morning, I sit at my beach front cottage, flanked on one side by a village of many very poor people, and on the other side, a church founded by Euro-Americans. It is Christmas Eve. The old man from the village exists from the rear of the church, walks about 50 ft away and lifts his cloth to piss in open and public view. This is the same man who repeats this motion every Sunday. By taking just a few more steps, he could have a private place to relieve himself. A few minutes later, three small girls, all under eight years, dressed in their Sunday best, come to almost the exact spot to openly stoop to relieve themselves. Fifteen minutes later, the same three girls are outside repeating the same behavior.

150

Even though I detest public urination, this particular church has two toilets, and I wonder if the Ghanaians are forbidden to use them because the toilets are for the exclusive use of the Euro-American missionaries. Or is the real problem perhaps that the villagers are not used to using the toilet, even though there is one public facility in that tiny village?

It is in this town, Elmina, Ghana, where Kwame Nkrumah began his mission to educate his Ghanaian people on their grand and noble history. He entreated them to join him in reclaiming that high Golden Stool upon which their ancestors sat. He began by teaching the children and the message of their royal past, their heroes who fought against the outside invaders and won. All their power and glory could be restored if they stood up against the outsiders and kindly asked them to leave their shores, to return to their native lands in Europe.

The great Osagyefo Dr. Kwame Nkrumah won the first two rounds. He liberated Ghana, even as he was held captive from behind prison walls. He was jailed for having the audacity to defy European rule. His bold move dislodged the whole of Africa and led to the liberation movement throughout the continent, the Caribbean Islands and Aboriginal Diaspora nations of South America. Those were the first two rounds.

The Europeans are clever, based on their inherent ability for long-term planning. Even before Dr. Nkrumah's inauguration, there was a long term plan for his overthrow with the ultimate plan for re-colonization of Africa. That plan was called Christian indoctrination.

Today in Ghana, the image of the white Christ dominates everything. The image is prevalent all over the streets and the marketplace, inside the businesses, the schools. The white *"Savior's"* image is on the windows of the taxicabs, the buses and the trucks. Everywhere you look, the white Christ, who looks nothing like the African people, looms over the entire culture with

151

the promise of *"salvation"* after death, somewhere in the *"bye-n-bye"*. The sad and pitiful sounds of the European imperialists' gospel songs (*even cowboy Christmas songs*) dominate the radio and television stations this Christmas day. The taxi drivers play gospel music instead of the cheerful and soulful *"high life music"* of independence movement and culture in Ghana. As king Leopold mandated of the Christian missionaries, they, the Europeans were the **"fathers over their** [African] **souls"** and they, the missionaries, should be obeyed and revered over and above obedience to their African parents, elected and traditional leaders and their ancestors.

Images have power over words because even the illiterate can see, and they are impressed by what they see. Words that they don't understand do not have the same impact. Hence, the image of the white Christ everywhere re-enforces white supremacy and African inferiority. **"A picture is worth a thousand words".**

What bothers me the most is that the Christian indoctrination inundates the schools, both the public and private, secular and religious educational institutions. The public school curriculum in Ghana mandates **"Religious and Moral Education"**. After reading several of these text books used in the schools, I determined that even this education is slanted toward Christianity, white supremacy and African ancestral disdain. There is a mention of Islam, as this religion has a sizable following in Ghana. **"Allah"** is not given the same status as **"God"**, although it is my understanding that Allah and God are one and the same and they are called by different names by the two religions. Traditional religious practices are spoken of with disrespect and contempt, using condescending words such as *"animist, fetish, juju, heathen and idolatry"* attached to those indigenous religions.

Foreign names, mostly English names, are taken by everyone. Children are taught in schools that it is very bad to

152

carry a name that suggests traditional beliefs, ancestral respect or ancestral spiritual names or practices. They are told that this is *"heathen"* and they will not go to heaven when they die. School children are kept in fear of *"sin"* that they will not be *"forgiven"*, and they are kept in fear of corporal punishment, even for the smallest and most nonsensical word, movement, misbehavior and short coming.

Christian indoctrination begins in nursery school, with *"born in sin"* being the focal point, that you are *"saved"* only because the *"white Christ suffered and died for your sins"*, and corporal punishment is the threat for non-conformance. Children are set up for a state of fear for which they are unable to escape for a life time.

Ghana after fifty years of independence has slipped down a very narrow slope into subservience and total obedience to their colonizers, those whom they perceive to be the sons and daughters of their *"Lord and Savior Jesus Christ"*, the white Europeans and Euro-Americans. My personal opinion is that they have less freedom than slaves on the American plantations during the olden days of slavery, and they do not believe that there is any hope or salvation for them except in death. They do not believe that they have any power to fight to free themselves because their only freedom is in the afterlife.

Hence, the weekend retreats are to funerals. Funerals are the most celebrated events on Ghana's social calendar. Funerals start as early as Thursday nights, but surely by Friday night, and they last through Sunday. Everybody goes to a funeral. There is much singing and dancing, eating, drinking and jubilation, because the departed souls have been released from their earthly bondage of *"sin"* and can now join the *"Lord and Savior Jesus Christ"* in heaven.

Osagyefo Dr. Kwame Nkrumah is crying buckets of tears for Ghana. He lies restless in his grave. His image is barely seen

153

in Ghana, for the *"white Christ"* has taken over the minds and hearts of the people. "**Osagyefo**" means, "**Savior**", and Nkrumah was indeed the "**Savior**" of Africa during the 1950's and early 60's. He instilled the people with pride, self respect and dignity, and reminded them of their true greatness. All of Africa followed. It took just a few dollar bills, a few bottles of whiskey, some cigarettes and a stupid soldier to bring down a whole people, because once "**Osagyefo**" was dethroned, the other selfish, self-serving, stupid generals were standing in line to take their turn for the crumbs, morsels and white prostitutes they traded to the colonial powers for their peoples' freedom and their country's wealth.

On a Ghana television news broadcast last week, a text message was read, which appeared to be from one of the **"old guard"** who remember Ghana's glory days. He too was crying buckets of tears because Ghana has given up on freedom and self reliance. The messenger lamented that even the university educated students do not know Ghana's national anthem.

I tested this comment by asking a well educated, articulate graduate if he knew the national anthem; he admitted that he didn't. This same well spoken, intelligent man truly believes that the Lord Jesus Christ died to save the world. When I told him that "**Osagyefo**" means "**Savior**", he argued me down that Kwame Nkrumah was not a "**Savior**". This man is not yet thirty years old, and Ghana's education system failed to give him the history of Ghana and the importance of Dr. Kwame Nkrumah's legacy. *What Ghana's educational system did for him was to indoctrinate him into Christianity and* **"White Supremacy."**

My heart is sad, though I have not given up. Like pioneers before me and pioneers to come, I will reach those who did not receive that *"school indoctrination"*, those who were too *"lowly and poor"* to afford an *"education"*. They are the ones who are brave enough and bold enough to stand up for themselves and to demand a better life. After all, they have nothing to loose, and they will fight for their dignity and to save their own lives.

Although King Leopold is leading right now there is a level of discontent among the masses. What they need is an inspired leader, an orator, a benevolent dictator, who will show them their greatness, and lead them to uncover it. Ghana's greatness has been shrouded in a cloak of shame and disrespect for self.

The late and great Aboriginal American historian, Dr. John Henrick Clarke, a friend and colleague to Osagyefo Nkrumah, wept for and grieved over the fall of his friend from power. His lamentation was that, at the celebration of Ghana's independence, on that fateful night when it was time to call for the blessing of the High Creator, there was a disturbance and disagreement among the leaders. There were those who wanted to pour libation and ask for the blessings of the ancestors, in the tradition of Ghana's ancient ways. There was the group that was ashamed of this ancestral custom, because of the presence of the Europeans, especially the Queen of England. They urged Osagyefo to call a Christian minister to say a prayer instead of pouring libation in Ghana's ancient tradition. Dr. Clarke believed that, when the ancestors' blessings were absconded, denied, their presence neglected and their dignity disregarded, this act was the very first step in the downfall of Ghana and Africa.

Until their place on the high alter among all the gods, the angels and the Universal Spirits is restored to its proper place, and the false gods and *"graven images"* have been removed from the throne, Ghana and Africa will continue to bow Her head in shame, and give away Her wealth and Her future to a foreign master.

Footnote: Attachment King Leopold's mandate to his missionaries King Leopold's Mandate (Thanks to Dr. Chiedozie Okoro) King Leopold's mandate to his missionaries and the passivity of Africans world-wide

155

Sofi, Gyasi, and Esi at Kwame Nkrumah's
Memorial, Accra, Ghana.

Ghana after Fifty Years – Part II
Chinweizu's Commentary on King Leopold's Mandate to the Missionaries

Please reflect especially on the 7 specific measures highlighted in the document:

1] Your action will be directed essentially to the younger ones, for they won't revolt when the recommendation of the priest is contradictory to their parent's teachings.

2] The children have to learn to obey what the missionary recommends, who is the father of their soul.

3] Teach students to read and not to reason

4] Teach the niggers to forget their heroes and to adore only ours.

5] You have to detach from them and make them disrespect everything which gives courage to affront us.

6] Institute a confessional system, which allows you to be good detectives denouncing any black that has a different consciousness contrary to that of the decision-maker.

7] You have to keep watch on dis-interesting our savages from the richness that is plenty [in their underground]. To avoid that they get interested in it, and make you murderous competition and dream one day to overthrow you. They are a recipe for turning Africans into *"niggers"* docile, non-rebellious and incapable of self-organized resistance to their white exploiters. Their successful implementation is sufficient to explain African passivity before white power.

We should note: 1] that all missionaries carried out, and still carry out, that mandate. We are only lucky to have found King Leopold's articulation of the aim of all Christian imperialist missionaries to Africa. 2] Even the African converts who today manage the older churches in Africa (the priests, bishops,

Archbishops, Cardinals etc of the Roman and Protestant sects), and especially also those who evangelize Born-Again Christianity, still serve the same mandate. Which is why they demonize African gods and Anglicize African names, and drop the names of African deities which form part of African names; and still attack and demolish the African shrines that have managed to survive, e.g. Okija. 3] Those Africans who voluntarily converted to Christianity before the colonial conquest *"such as Affonso I of the Ba Kongo in the 15th century"* probably did not discern the purpose of the brand of Christianity that was supplied to them. This was probably why they fell easy prey to the missionaries and the white traders and pirates who followed them.

But their Japanese counterparts probably did discern the game, even without access to some version of Leopold's letter. But even if the **Japanese Shoguns** did not intuit what Leopold makes explicit, they clearly realized the danger of Japanese converts to Christianity forming a fifth column within Japanese society and state, a fifth column loyal to their *co-revisionists* in Europe. To rid Japan of that danger, in the late 16th century, the Shoguns began their expulsion of Portuguese and Spanish missionaries on the grounds that they were forcing Japanese to become Christian, teaching their disciples to wreck temples, taking and trading slaves, etc. Then, in 1596, it became clear to the Japanese authorities that *Christianization* had been a prelude to Spanish conquest of other lands; and it quickly dawned on them that a fifth column loyal to Rome and controlled by the priests of a foreign religion was a clear and present danger to the sovereignty of a newly unified Japan. Soon after, the persecution and suppression of Japanese Christians began. Early in the 17th century, sensing the danger from a creed that taught obedience to foreign priests rather than the Japanese authorities, all missionaries were ordered to leave and all Japanese were ordered to register at the Buddhist temples. When Japanese Christians took part in a rebellion, foreign priests were executed, the Spanish were expelled and Japanese Christians were forbidden to travel abroad. After another rebellion, largely by Christians, was put down, the Japanese Christians were suppressed and their descendants were put under close state surveillance for centuries thereafter. In the 1640s all Japanese suspected of being Christians were ruthlessly exterminated. Thus did Japan, by 1650, save itself from the first European attempt to mentally subvert, conquer and colonize it. 4] The African captives who were taken abroad and enslaved, and the Africans at home after the European conquest, having already been forcibly deprived of their autonomy, were in no political position to resist Christianization. Thus the Christianity still practiced in all of the Aboriginal American Diaspora, just as that in the African homeland since the start of the 20th century, continues to carry out the Leopoldian mandate. Hence, for example, whereas the White Born-Again of the USA, when in US Navy ships in WWII, sang: "Praise the Lord, and pass the ammunition,"the attitude of African Born-Again converts today is best summed up as: "Praise **the Lord, and lie down for the manna**."Thanks to a century or more of this Leopold-mandated missionary mind control, African Christians are not an activist, self-helping, politically engaged and resolute, let alone militant bunch. Hence their putting up with all manner of mistreatment and exploitation by their mis-rulers, white and black. The most they are disposed to do to their mis-rulers is to admonish them to *"Fear God "*as one protester's miserable placard read in the last Lagos demonstration against the latest of the murderous fuel price hikes by the present Misgovernment. The idea of an uprising to tame their mis-rulers is alien to the religiously opiated frame of mind of the Nigerians. 5] The lesson in the contrast between an Africa that the Christian missionaries brainwashed and subverted, and a Japan where this brainwashing and subversion was forcibly prevented, is stark and clear. What then must Africans of today begin to do to save themselves from brainwashing by their *"White World enemies here on earth?"* That is the question.**--Chinweizu**

1.Chinweizu is a Nigerian scholar, commentator and Pan African Nationalist. He gave a paper at the Aboriginal Heritage Summit Plenary Talk, *"Compradorism: The Problem with African Leadership"* in Lagos NIIH. The article was posted on the web on January 3, 2007.

Ibekwe Chinweizu
Author, Journalist, and Essayist

Compradors & Compradorism
The Agenda of the Negro and African
Disciples of White Supremacy

Sometimes I wish I could just mind my own business, and leave the world to its own course. That is the easy way out, and many choose this option. I have always been concerned about others, especially those who are in greater need than I am. All African people or Aboriginal people don't feel that way. I remember about 15 years ago, I was talking to a young Nigerian boy, the "*god son*" of a friend, who was attending school in Atlanta. His greatest ambition was to hurry to finish his University education so that he could "*become a minister of oil or finances in Nigeria and steal some of the money*". These were his actual, truthful words, his ambitions, his goals in life.

The boy was about 19 years old, and I wondered what ever happened to youthful enthusiasm, concern for others and desire to do good and to make a positive impact and contributions in life. I wondered how this young boy could become so selfish, so self-centered at such a young and tender age. What we see in this child is the makings of what Nigerian scholar, Chinweizu[1] calls, *Compradors,* the African who is the fifth pillar in the continued exploitation of Africa, Her people, Her natural and mineral resources and Her human resources. These "*Compradors*" are the enemy within, who stand at the gate and allow these enemies of Africa full and continued access to Africa's wealth. These, gatekeepers, the "*Disciples of White Supremacy*", do damage to Africa all in the name of their own personal gain of wealth and influence, for the wealth of their individual families and the approval of their masters.

Over the past year, living in Ghana, I am seeing this side of life that I was aware of, and I kept away from it because I don't

161

want to take part in these activities. What is it? It is the activity of *"selling out"* the future progress of an entire group of people for one's own selfish gain or for one's own family advancement. Since I had witnessed these same activities on a local level in the southern town where I was born, all the way to the national level, where the so called *"civil rights leaders"* continue to *"sell out"* the future of the Aboriginal race in America for their own personal gain, or for their individual family's gain. One such opportunist comes to mind, who called for a national boycott of a certain beer company. He called off the boycott when his son was awarded a beer distribution contract. Surely, he can be marked as an enemy of the people. Yet, he is still respected as a *"civil rights leader"*.

I know that these same kind of *"sell outs"* are the reason for the failure of African states. From the assassination of Patrice Lumumba and the overthrow of Kwame Nkrumah by western power interests as well as the western powers' covert support of rogue armies such as Julius Sivimbi's in Angola. What I didn't know is that this same disloyalty and self-centered greed reaches all the way down to the small villages of Africa, where exploitation of the poor is rampant among the elite, often educated, sometimes inherited (*chieftaincy* and *kingship*) leaders.

This is not a judgment on all African or Aboriginal American leadership. I am simply sharing my concerns and observations, because I have experienced this anomaly up close and far too often in my sojourn in Ghana. I have found myself mumbling in disbelief of some of the things that people do, and how because of it, it is so difficult to implement change, even much needed changes in some communities. It is the social structure, the tiered status, power and influence peddling that stands in the way of progress.

Take, for instance, the situation of water in my village. The municipal water pipe flows through the village, but it is turned off most of the time. What I have witnessed is that the water company

162

turns the water on, perhaps one of two days a month, to allow for just enough water to pass through the meter to register usage. This results in the generation of a water bill, to bring about a basic charge to generate the money to pay for the new water pipeline.

Massive human resources are wasted daily securing water for household use. I see children as young as four and five years old carry heavy loads of water on their heads, for preparing the family's food, bathing and washing clothes. Some wake up as early as 4 AM, while I see other children traveling the roads in the dark of night. Women with a load at the front, pregnant, with a child at the back and 5 gallons of water on their heads walk for miles to secure this precious commodity. It pains me to see this drudgery day in and day out.

People in the village with moderate resources have acquired a personal water holding tank, and they buy water from the same municipal service that should be supplying pipe water to everyone. The cost of the tank, alone, is equal to six months' salary for many residents, and filling the tank can cost half of one month's salary. So you can see how impossible it is for the ordinary Ghanaian to buy water this way.

I asked one of the villages' elders and opinion leaders what could be done to address this situation. He informed me that there was already a plan in place to build a water holding reservoir for providing water when there is no municipal pipe water flowing. The elder said that a local business had donated 300 cement blocks and 8 bags of cement to build the reservoir, but since that was not enough, all the materials were just sitting there, and nothing was being done to address the water problem.

In my opinion, there was a very easy way to address this problem; that is, to raise money to complete the building of the reservoir. To me, this was too simple an obstacle to stand in the way of supplying 200 village people access to water each day.

I went to work, appealing to friends, relatives, customers

163

and business associates, to assist me by donating this small amount of money to purchase materials to build the reservoir. I received immediate responses from people, and I soon had enough money to buy the necessary materials to complete the reservoir. From my end, I pushed every one of the village craftsmen involved in the construction, to hurry to complete the task. I stayed on the carpenter's case, I appealed to the stone mason, I coerced and urged the truck driver, to pick up and deliver the materials, I begged the young boys involved in the *G.E.N.E.S.I.S.* Project, to supply the labor to deliver the sand from the beach to the building site, and to transport the donated rocks, left over from the construction of my water tower from my house to the building site. My desire was to see the water reservoir constructed and filled with water.

The work went fast at first; then the pace began to slow. As completion became imminent, every conceivable excuse possible was given by the mason, why he was unable to complete the work. He even resorted to telling a story about how, some time ago, he was *"cursed"* by a jealous competitor who wanted his job. Because of this "**curse**", every time he touched cement he would get sick. The only remaining work to conclude the construction was some finishing touches to be completed by a mason. However, the project was stuck! No one was moving, and I became suspicious; it is my nature to question because I am optimistic, practical and cautious, all at the same time.

I wasn't absolutely certain what the delay was, and who was benefiting by the delay. I only knew that everyone in the village had the daily chore of fetching water. The only relief anyone got from that chore, came when I had to fill my own water tank.

Each time my 1100 gallon water tank was empty, I called the municipal water company, and they sent a water tanker to fill the tank. It was at these times, every 7-10 days, when the villagers see the tanker at my house, they would all rush with every description of container, from a two gallon bucket to a twenty gallon plastic barrel. They would all run to my house to fill their receptacles. Even though others in the neighborhood received water delivery service, the villagers only came to fetch water when it was delivered to my house.

This was not a problem for me, because when I buy the water, I pay for the entire truck load of water. Hence, the water left over after filling my tank, would only be sold again. I was happy to share.

Announcement came that the Chief Executive of the area, would visit the village to hear about the villages' concerns. Fortunately, the local representative, our Assemblyman, sent word to inform me of the visit. I would show up, to keep informed, and to ask publicly, what the hold up was on completion of the reservoir. I do not speak the language, and all deliberations are in the local Fanti language. But because certain English words are interjected, as there are no indigenous words to substitute, one can understand what topics are being discussed, even if the details of the discussion are not surmised.

The meeting started three hours later, *African time*, and the formalities proceeded. I always admire the civility of community meetings and assemblies. Acknowledgement of the elders and leaders comes first, always with great respect and humility. After these formalities, the spokesperson for the Royal family, the Okyeame, rose to speak on behalf of the community, to inform the Chief Executive of the needs of the people.

First on the list of complaints was water. The speaker was requesting two Poly-tanks for the village, to provide water when the pipe was not flowing. I was shocked and surprised that the elder was reporting that the reason for the water problem in the village was the lack of a water receptacle. There were protests from the audience, from villagers who knew that there was a receptacle in the village for holding water. The elders, all men, sitting in the front row, hushed all audience participation, and refused to allow

165

other voices to be heard. I was seated on the platform with the Chief Executive and Assembly-man. I had a bird's eye view of what was happening in the audience. Many protest voices attempted to refute the elders; all voices were squashed!

The Chief Executive spoke of the difficulties in securing water flow because of the building of the new water pipe. He guaranteed that water would flow in the pipes by November. These are the same predictions I heard about the water pipe one year ago, that in six months, the new pipe would be completed. No matter who is reporting about the completion of the new water pipe, it is promised in six months time. He talked about the cost of a Poly-tank, and how the cost of this water holding tank is prohibitive. He promised, however, that if such a tank was available, he would send the municipal water provider to the village to fill the tank for the people to use.

There was one brave woman who stood up, and in the local language, accused the elders of conducting community business in secret. She urged the inclusion of a woman among the elders, so there would be transparency and the village would know what was going on, and what the elders were planning for community development. There was uproar of approval for the bravery of the woman who put her reputation and community standing in jeopardy by publicly condemning the elders. Even though I did not understand her words, I understood her passion and her sincere concern.

The time was getting late, and I began to wonder if I would be given the platform to talk about the **G.E.N.E.S.I.S. Projects** (*Growing Energy & Nutrition for Environment Stability & Investments in our Societies*). Finally, just as the sun was descending over the western horizon, the village "*wunnube*" elder-in-waiting, who helped with the water reservoir, was forced to acknowledge my presence, and to also acknowledge the presence and near completion of the water reservoir in the village. The

166

Assemblyman asked if I had a few words to add, and I got up to speak.

I thanked the woman who talked so passionately. Even though I did not understand her words, I was later told what she said. I then proceeded to say that, water would have been in the village yesterday, if the reservoir was completed. I bought water from the municipal water tanker yesterday. At least 30 villagers, women and children, descended upon my house to fill their containers. Because there was water left over in the tanker, that water could have been sent to the village to fill the reservoir.

My announcement to the community was news to many, because those who should be informing the people, apparently, had ulterior motives, selfish interest, secret agendas which they want to protect. Hence, the presence of an answer to their major community complaint, i.e., lack of water, stumped their efforts to secure monies for the Poly-tanks.

It was apparent that their plan has been to hoard that money for personal gains. Therefore, if the community provided a water tank through their own collective efforts, the need for the district assembly to allocate funds for the purchase of a water holding tank was no longer necessary. This did not fit into the elders' plans and personal agendas.

Self reliance, self-sufficiency, innovation, creativity, and solving societal problems through creative community projects, does not fit into the agenda of the **Compradors**. Their job is to keep the people in need, begging for crumbs, never finding satisfaction in cooperative projects and collective innovation. Dependency on the Compradors' leadership, and their white supremacist benefactors, fosters the perpetual state of despair and disenfranchisement that keeps the enemies of Africa in power, and their Comprador enablers rich. With the assistance of their white supremacist benefactors, these Compradors wield a long, wicked cane, always threatening anyone who has the audacity to question

167

their authority over the future of the people they "*lead.*"

What I want for the people is not necessarily what the leaders want for the people. Just think, if the women and children had three extra hours each day to think, study, plan, read or discuss issues, they may very well stand up and oppose the decisions and actions taken by the elders, those decisions that go against the community's best interest. If the women and children had three extra hours each day, and were not totally drained by the trek in the scorching sun to fetch water, they may plan to take over their gold mines, their diamond mines, their bauxite mines, their timber industry, their abundant food crops, their fisheries, their damns and their schools.

What would then become of the elders, the appointed leaders, the Compradors and their white supremacy masters', world domination, African subjugation and African extermination agenda?

I may have stepped into a caldron of boiling water by suggesting that change can be seen on the village level in Ghana. **Change is not in the interest of the "*powers that be.*"** The planned subjugation of Africa must be achieved quickly within a few years by the **"*globalization propagandist.*"** Otherwise, the common people might find enough water to dilute the clouds in their brains, and rise up to demand the return of their country from the hands of the white supremacist and the greatest enemy from within, the Compradors! Compradors, look out!

Compradors and Compradorism
Part II

*"When the men go off to war, the lame stand up,
dust themselves off,
and take over the village leadership."*
Akan proverb

The brain drain in Africa is so pronounced, that one can easily see why the continent continues to mark time, and in many cases, move backwards. To cause a change in attitudes, beliefs and habits is a monumental task. It is for this reason that the bravest, the strongest, the most intelligent and the most adventurous individuals leave their homes for unknown destinations in search of a chance, an opportunity to move in another direction. Hence, every city or progressive capital in every westernized country, including Europe, Asia and North America, have seen an influx of African people from almost every African nation. They enter these countries through every means they can manage, legally, as students, tourists, and illegally, sometimes as stowaways on boats and trucks, over borders, through ports and on foot.

One might even suggest that this practice is not new because during the trans-Atlantic slave trade, those who were selected to be transported mostly to Brazil and South America in the Americas were usually the most fit, the strongest, able bodied. Many who were captured in local wars were the soldiers. So it is safe to say that for the last 500 years, Africa has been loosing the *"cream of the crop"* of future, able bodied leaders.

Back in the days of Kwame Nkrumah, Namdi Azikawe and Jomo Kenyatta, all of them left their homes for studies abroad; but they returned to initiate change. When they returned, they found the same people in charge, those who benefited from the colonial presence, the status quo, the elite, and the selected and inherited leaders, the Compradors. In spite of the odds, these brave Africans took on the battle, and because the masses of people were still innocent of western ways and materialism, they were able to secure their enthusiastic support for independence and change.

Nowadays, western culture and values, material greed, and especially western religions, have separated the African people from themselves. Africans have abandoned so many of the traditions that kept them honest and their moves and motives honorable. Families have broken down and are in a state of dysfunction, much the same as the American families. The masses of people have been turned into paupers and beggars, even those in the respectable middle class of government and educational institutions. Everyone is on the take for whatever they can get from anyone they can con.

I am not painting everyone with the same brush. Like everything else, this description speaks about many, but not everyone. On almost every level of government and social status, from farm worker to taxi driver to electricity office worker to business owner to preacher to school teacher to postal worker to community opinion makers to chiefs to Members of Parliament and the Presidency, in many African nations, there is corruption. Because the wages are so low, and the cost of living in the modern world is so high, to enjoy the wonders of the western culture, TV, videos, cars, refrigerators, these otherwise honest and sincere people, have to stoop to the level of thief and con artist, to enjoy these western *"wonders"*. On the middle class, civil service level their integrity is often compromised just to send their children to school.

As the bold and brave ones grow into adulthood, they see no hope for a future of prosperity, advancement and change; hence, they go to every extent to move away from their homes to travel to any city outside of Africa. What is left at home are those who were not as bold, who were not willing to risk everything to the unknown, who were not as clever or adventurous; sometimes they just could not get enough money together, through honest means, to travel someplace else. The children of the elite, whose inherited position in the society is clear cut and assured, after completing their studies abroad, they return to take over their inherited leadership positions. Africa is left with the **"cripples"**, the beggars, the petty thieves and the elite.

What is most disturbing is that, when an African wants to return home from abroad, because of the love of his country, his success abroad or retirement he encounters so many obstacles that he sometimes gives up and goes back to his adopted nation. Only a few are bold and brave enough, like Kwame Nkrumah, to face the opposition and drive the course home. It is just too difficult to fight the power of the elite and the jealousy and envy of the *"cripples"* who stayed behind. The *"cripples"* have now joined the ranks of the Compradors. Those at the middle and bottom realm of society have become a part of the elite and the government officials who keep the doors open for Africa's exploitation. In civil service, because of the fear of their own incompetence, or the fear that they will be passed over for promotion or advancement, they stand in the way of their own progress and the progress of the nation as a whole. The *"returnee"* doesn't stand a chance of making needed changes or implementing new ideas.

On every level of society, the returnee is exploited; the taxi driver will charge him more, the store keeper will charge him more, the tailors and seamstresses will charge him more, the plumbers will charge him more, the electrician will charge him more and every service that he applies for will demand a bribe. Africa is frozen in the Colonial past.

It is for this reason that the **Colonial *"masters"*** have been able to take back Africa so easily. The Compradors would rather see a white man in charge on any and every level of society, than to see his own brother, a *"been-to"* (**one's countryman who has been-to the West**) come back to serve as a leader or to participate in change. Much of this is the result of Christian *"brainwashing"*, which has convinced the Africans on every level of society, that every white man is the direct descendant of their lord and savior, Jesus Christ.

So who is at fault, what is the fault, how can we address these issues? It seems almost a lost cause, because it takes a big storm to stir up enough momentum to undo stagnation. Perhaps it is the *"hunter and gatherer mentality"* that keeps change at bay. When you look for your food and water daily, and you don't plan for your food and water for next year, you never have the time to change anything, because your entire focus is on today's food. Planning takes time and peace of mind.

So we look for the storm to stir up the stagnation. But the *"hunter and gatherer"* many times will move to another place rather than to stay put and find a solution to the problem. In today's world, finding a solution too often means staging another trick or con game for the next innocent victim who comes along.

We pray for the storm to stir up the stagnation in Africa's consciousness, so that She can begin a new life to enjoy the fruits of the Good Earth that the Great Spirit blessed Her with so abundantly. **God gave Mother Africa everything.** *Now She must find and believe in Her own strength.*

Marcus Garvey, the Godfather of the 20th Century *"Return to Africa"* movement, said that we would find him in the *"whirlwind"*. **Bring on the** *"whirlwind"*, **bring on the** *"whirlwind"*!

Compradors and Compradorism – Part III

There seems no end to the stories about the negative **effects of the Compradors** upon the African Society. The Compradors, those who stay in their countries and act as agents of European dominance, what I call *"Negro disciples of white supremacy"*, continue to take Africa backwards into colonial days. They immobilize every effort to bring progress to an area, usually for their own advancement and monetary greed. However, if their activities at the village level are not recognized and rooted out, there can be no hope for the restoration of the African people to their lands, their wealth, their culture and even their own minds.

The politics of water is the most disturbing to me. Water is more important to survival than food; a person can live much longer without food than he can live without water.

Yet water continues to be the item that commands the continuous efforts of women and children every single morning and every single evening in every part of Ghana. I see them in the morning when I take a walk; I see them in the evening when I return from the farm. All the time I see them carrying the 4 gallon yellow plastic jug and every other description of tub and container.

I personally felt that I could make a small effort in the community I live in, so I took over a project which lay dormant in that village for months. Materials had been purchased to build a water reservoir in the village, but it was not enough. I asked for donations from friend and customers in America to complete the project. Within a short time, the necessary money was collected.

The local Compradors stood in the way of the completion of the reservoir (See *Compradors & Compradorism-Part I*). Finally, after the finishing touches were completed members of the **G.E.N.E.S.I.S. Project** sat down to figure out how much water the reservoir could hold and the cost of filling it. This information was necessary in order to determine what the community would have to charge per bucket of water to realize enough money to continue to keep a water supply flowing in the village. The village would also have to select a person to be in charge of collecting and holding the money, a person of integrity who everyone trusted to serve the community.

I traveled to Accra one weekend; I returned to find that the reservoir had been filled. Who filled it and who is in charge of collecting the money? Well, it didn't take long to discover what had transpired. The **Grand Comprador #1** in the village was sitting at the side of the reservoir collecting the fees for the water. This man, a leading opinion-maker in the village, and his wife were in charge. I wondered where he got the money to fill the tank and who appointed him to serve as banker?

To uncover the mystery I went to the business owner who donated the first materials. After a long talk with them, it was discovered that the Grand Comprador of the village was playing a nasty game. Each time that **G.E.N.E.S.I.S.** bought materials for the reservoir, i.e., cement, iron rods, wood for framing, this thief would take receipts to the business donor and claim that he had just purchased those materials that we had purchased. He would then be reimbursed for the materials and the monies would disappear into his personal wallet.

It is not hard to get receipts from most businesses. It just takes a little *"dash"* to the sales clerk. After all, almost all transactions are in cash and there is no one checking the receipts. Therefore, cash money in the clerks hand gives you a receipt for any amount you want to claim. The clerk's pay is so small that any amount of *"dash"* will help him with his daily food.
In the final analysis, the business that donated money to begin the reservoir project actually believed that they had paid for the construction of the entire reservoir. That business also donated the

money to fill the reservoir. However, all the money that was given to the Grand Comprador was *"chopped"*; the money went solely to his pocket. Not one *pesewa* went to the completion of the reservoir! The business owner and I met with a respected Elder in the village. We told him about what had transpired. He was shocked! The business owner also revealed that monies had also been donated, and given to the Grand Comprador for village improvements that were never realized. This really upset the Elder!
Therefore, a meeting was planned in two weeks, after the Elder informed other elders of this theft of community resources.

Time has passed. I have not heard from the Elder. I have not heard from the business owner, who also donated the funds to fill the reservoir the first time. The reservoir is empty; no one knows what happened to the money that was collected with the first filling of the reservoir. Apparently, this money was also *"chopped"* by the Grand Comprador; he placed himself in charge.

I will again intervene at the appropriate time. The reservoir is like a *"white elephant"* right now. The rains come enough so that water can be collected from the rooftops. The aluminum roofing sheets are coated with asbestos, for what reason I do not know, except perhaps to slowly poison the people. But they do not know that the roofing sheets are poison.

It is my hope that the people in the village will not act like the vulture, who sits in the rain and vows to build a nest to keep dry; then the next day when the sun comes out, the vulture says that really, he doesn't need a nest because look at this bright sunshine!

I can not close my eyes to the evil that lurks around me. I can not pretend that all is well when the majority suffers and the few enjoy. My heart bleeds. I can not look to the light and pretend that the darkness is not there.

175

Compradors and Compradorism -- Part IV
Ignorance is not Bliss

Now that the Central Region of Ghana, in particular the towns of Elmina and Cape Coast, have had electricity service almost uninterrupted for more than a week, I have had the opportunity to tune into local television programs. I just about gave up on watching the Evening News on all local stations, and because there is very little international news after 5:00 PM, my television stays in the mute position or completely off until about 10PM. At this time some of the real issues concerning the state of affairs in Ghana are discussed, often with guest speakers with opposing views to the present regime.

Sunday night I was looking for something interesting to watch and found nothing but sports, dancing and singing. Then there was an interview, which caught my attention. An economist, Dr. Nii Thompson, was talking about the lack of development in Ghana over the past eight years of the present regime. Government corruption is at the helm of the lack of development. What is so evident is that the level of corruption is so acute that almost no funds for local improvements arrive at their destination. Funding for schools in outlying districts is usually spent in Accra. For instance, television sets are ordered for school districts that are not wired for electricity. Those TV sets usually end up in the homes of the ministers and the school administrators. School buildings for districts, if they are ever built, are usually of such poor quality of construction, due to the siphoning off of building materials by the administrative and/or government leaders. When construction is completed the buildings are often rejected by the districts. The funding designated for school furnishing, desks, chairs and blackboards never arrive at the schools, but are often diverted to private schools with the monies going into the pockets of administrators and government officials.

One example that Dr. Thompson gave really made me annoyed. There has been a great loss of life and property in one of the Northern regions of Ghana due to torrential rains. Roads and bridges are washed away, and thousands of people are homeless because of the flooding. The Evening News reported that the only cement factory in Ghana, **Ghacem**, a European owned company, donated 2,000 bags of cement to the entire disaster area.

The donation seemed like a noble and humanitarian gesture until I heard Dr. Thompson reveal that this same company, Ghacem, gives monthly bribes of 2,000 bags of cement to several government officials to keep out other cement factories and competition, so that their company continues the monopoly on this basic building material. The last time I bought cement I paid Gh ¢9.50, nine Ghana cedis, which is equal to $9.70 (nine dollars and seventy cents). I can buy three bags of cement in US for the same amount of money. The total donation for an entire disaster area of many square miles is less than ¢Gh20,000. This amount is only a fraction of what the company pays in bribes to Ghana officials to keep their exclusive business advantage.

But because Ghacem can bribe government officials and continue their monopoly in Ghana, they dictate the price and the public can do nothing about it. In fact, most people never heard this revelation. A local friend, a young man whom I talk to about Ghana government, tells me that most people never hear about these revelations, because when this information and discussions are televised most people are already asleep because they have to go to work the next day.

Another factor that keeps the people in the dark about government corruption is that this programming discussion is usually in English. All this is okay for me and other foreigners, but according to Dr. Thompson, 40% of the population of Ghana is illiterate and most of that population speaks very little English. Another 20% of the populace has a primary school education, and

177

can read to write, but not to the level of understanding to comprehend government corruption.

This is another factor that contributes to Ghana's underdevelopment. Hence, there is only 40% of Ghana's people can comprehend what is going on. Of that 40%, only 10% have a university education; this segment belongs to the ruling elite class. The remaining 30% is employed in the government segment. It is this 40% that benefits from the corruption, from the government ministers, Members of Parliament, Regional Ministers. Whatever is left over is devoured by the administrators of the various government agencies such as electricity, water, roads and education institutions. After all, the example of leadership only encourages the greed and corruption of the local leadership.

Therefore, ignorance is not bliss. Ignorance means exploitation of the underclass, leaving them in poverty and despair. I do wonder how the government officials sleep at night. It is likely that they fall into bed, inebriated, drugged with a stomach full of imported foods, topped of with pharmaceutical chemicals to make their bodies accept these foreign goods. How do we overcome these conditions; they can not last forever. Meanwhile, a new front will arise from the underclass, a new front that is tired of loosing everything to the few privileged at the top, the elite and the civil servants. Their time will come.

Dr. Nii Moi Thompson – Ghanaian Economist

Osagyefo Dr. Kwamah Nkrumah, 1st President

The Iron Benders & Stone Masons
Skills Preserved from Ancient Times
by African Craftsmen and Builders

After many years of watching pre-fabricated-factory assembled houses constructed and completed within five days in America, it has been quite a treat to see steel and stone foundations structured by hand, expertise that is carried over by craftsmen with the skills from ancient days. I have the pleasure of watching this craftsmanship unfold at my doorstep, while listening to the waves crashing against the rocks at my front door.

A steady and reliable access to water is a real challenge in this village. If you want water each time you turn on the faucet, you have to erect your own water tower. At times during the dry season, water does not run in the water pipes supplied by the municipality for days, and sometimes there is no water for weeks. Therefore, people are left to their own resources, and have to obtain water from wherever they can find it.

For most villagers, this means carrying water on their heads for long distances. This can be a real chore. For those with just moderate financial resources, they are able to purchase a water holding tank to supply a steady water source. The water tower is constructed high over the residence, to assure enough pressure to force the water to the desired areas of the house, the kitchen and the bathroom.

Construction of these high towers takes great skill. This is an even greater challenge when a tower is being constructed close the ocean. The torrential tropical rains and high winds, thunder and lightening bolts that accompany these storms roaring in from the ocean, and the constant high humidity and salty air, is a hazard to almost any structure. However, I have seen many of these towers and buildings stand quite well, even under these adverse conditions.

This is truly a testament to the solid workmanship that goes into these towers, and I wonder if the prefabricated houses that are being built close to my home in suburban Atlanta could withstand these conditions. I don't believe that the factory made houses could last even one year on this tropical shore. I remember one storm that hit South Atlanta that caused several of the newly constructed houses to spring leaks, loose roof-tops and crack siding, and I felt real compassion for the people who had just mortgaged their lives for 30 years to buy a house for $180,000.00, knowing that after 30 years the total payment could reach at least $500,000.00. This figure, of course, does not include repairs and maintenance, new roofs property taxes and new appliances.

While talking to the stone mason one day, he told me that some of the mud and thatched roof huts in old Elmina town and Iture village have stood for more than 200 years. I am told that this area where I am staying has been in existence for the last 500 years! I still don't understand how a mud house can withstand the torrential rains and high winds of these tropical storms. So I beg to wonder how the *Great Spirit* has favored the simplicity of life and closeness to Nature maintained by the inhabitants.

Even though there are water challenges and many other utility problems, especially the electricity supply that we take for granted in America, I choose to face these shortcomings. I have found a peace of mind, I sleep soundly at night, and I don't fear being the victim of racial profiling when I walk or ride down the street, minding my own business.

I am grateful for the slow process of steel and cement construction, the iron benders and the stone masons, because at the end of this gradual building procedure, there is a structure that will withstand the ravages of Mother Nature for centuries.

Stone Masons and Iron Benders build water towers and structures.

The African Mind

I was totally distraught. A virus took hold of my laptop and began to prompt me to delete files. On that particular day, I was a little off balance because I was in an automobile accident, where a car was passing illegally on a two lane highway. I was making a left turn into a gasoline service station. In my rear view and side view mirrors, I clearly saw the two cars directly behind me. The car had to be the third or fourth behind them and it was going at a high speed. It hit the left front side of the car, tearing of the fender and the lights. I was shaken up emotionally and psychologically, but not physically hurt.

I came home to write about my frustration (*see No Redress*) and the virus prompter began to work overtime. Without giving it much critical thought, I began to follow the instructions given by the antivirus scanner. Before I knew what was happening, my whole computer was dysfunctional. Nothing was working; I couldn't pull up any files or print any document or go online to use the internet. I worked until the wee hours, but the laptop function worsened.

What was I going to do! Here I am in a small town, Elmina, Ghana with the closest available technical help in a slightly larger town of Cape Coast. One day, I searched for a blank CD for two hours in Cape Coast. I couldn't find one, even at the computer school. I knew that I was in trouble because technological help like I needed to repair my laptop would be a two hour drive to Accra, the capital city.

I was especially hurt that I had lost many of the short stories I wrote, because I did not back up my work on an external disc. Three days after this loss, I was returning home after spending three hours in a hotel business center. A friend was approaching the house; she was coming for her mobile phone that was charging at my house.

I explained my predicament to her. She told me that her

184

teacher could repair it. I said, are you sure? Everyone told me that I had to go to Accra! She called her teacher; he was still at the school. We got into the car and drove to Cape Coast with the laptop.

We met Mr. Alfred as we climbed the stairs of a dilapidated building, three flights up. It was the same school where I couldn't find a blank CD six months ago. Mr. Alfred was a young, pleasant man. We sat down in the computer lab. The equipment was from the early 1990's; it looked like second hand computers sent from the progressive (*mostly white*) high schools to the ghetto schools in the USA. Mr. Alfred was very confident that I didn't have any problem that he could not handle. I was not too sure, because I was told by many people that such a technical computer problem could only be solved in Accra.

Mr. Alfred took the laptop and turned it on. He asked me about two questions and went to work. Within five minutes, he had retrieved my documents. I was ecstatic to see the many titles that I was so afraid that I had lost. But my problems were not over yet. Now a pathway had to be created whereby my documents could be transferred and saved in another area, and my laptop could be restored to a working condition.

Mr. Alfred worked on many levels, trying different computer pathways and using a language that I didn't understand. He worked vigorously, trying different approaches and using several CD's used in repairing software; well, this is what I thought he was doing, but I don't have that technical savvy.

Another teacher arrived to ask Mr. Alfred about some problem he was having. Mr. Alfred told him about my laptop problem, and they began to put their minds together. There were several options, they told me, how I could save my documents and install another operating system, or I could wipe my hard disc clean

185

and re-install the entire computer program as it came from the factory by using my recovery disc.

Because of time constraints and fear that I might loose my documents, I chose the option to install a second operating-system, and then later on, re-install the entire program. The two men worked together. There was no doubt that they knew what they were doing. Within four hours of my arrival at the school, my laptop was fully functional, my documents were all in tact and all the viruses on the laptop and pin drive were totally destroyed. I was on my way back to Elmina, about five miles down the road.

The African mind, with primitive tools and no new software, was able to restore this highly technical equipment of the modern world in a short time. Because none of the teachers had ever seen a brand new software like my Microsoft Office Suite, I promised that I would buy a new one, the latest version, and donate it to the school.

Ghana just struck oil last week. Gold has been mined in Ghana for centuries. Diamonds have been mined for centuries; yet the African minds are not given those tools that will propel them into the forefront of the twenty first century. **What's wrong with this picture?**

Visitors to Moringa Farm Kambon and Harris Families

Playing Football by the Ocean and the Danger of Losing the Ball to the Waves

Training Grounds for the Future Black Stars

At the height of the gathering, I counted 21 boys, mostly teens, some a little younger, maybe one or two over 18 years. They gathered in the grassy knoll of a white American missionary church yard which was deserted and left in the hands of locals. But that's another story.

The weather was balmy in the late afternoon. After the stinging rays of the equatorial sun subsided, the breeze of the Atlantic Ocean ascended. My beloved ocean front cottage lies next door to this Christian mission. I was sitting on the screened veranda (*we call it a porch in the old south*), watching the ocean waves, after a busy afternoon connecting with business interests in the USA.

The boys descended on the church grounds with a thunderous roar. They were excited about kicking the soccer ball around in a suitable, flat field. It was a safe area. Half of them wore shoes, some wore only socks, and others were bare foot. These disparities made no difference to them. They were ready to play.

There were no goal posts, no net, and the stadium "*seating*" was the ocean front. Only the waves and I bore witness to the game. It was apparent that the object was to kick the ball around with as much skill and power as any could muster. The game was on!

I noticed that a young father had joined the group. He was sitting on the sidelines, on the back steps of the church, with his two year old daughter climbing all over him. He was patient and attentive; he seemed not at all perturbed at the presence of the baby. Later on, I noticed that some of the smaller boys, not yet teens, took over the care of the baby girl; they were riding her on their backs. Meanwhile, the young father had joined the game. *"It takes a*

188

village to raise a child", an African proverb, is more than a catchy phase on the African continent.

The excitement of the nation of Ghana's *"Black Stars"* **Soccer Team,** actually qualifying for the semi-finals in the World Cup Soccer Games in Germany had infested the nation. In fact, the whole of Africa was proud of Ghana's achievement. There was jubilation throughout the nation and around the continent. Nigeria was ecstatic; Senegal was jubilant; South Africa was celebrating. Naturally, every young boy in Ghana dreamed of becoming the next super-star football (soccer) player, with the hopes of climbing out of what he perceived to be a life of hopelessness, poverty and despair. They were all honing their skills.

It took great dexterity to kick the ball around, while avoiding the ocean. These youngsters were pretty good at it. Most of them lived in the village just across an open field from my cottage. They, also, shared the ocean as their front yard. Their tiny huts were small, even compared to mine; some lived in mud huts with thatch roofs.

None of these differences mattered while the game was on. All were vying for the ball! Hit it any way you can, with your foot, head, chest, shoulder, behind. Just hit it, being careful not to break the official rules of the soccer game!

The clash was on; the ball moved backwards and forwards, kicked with bare feet, diverted with a single hard blow from the head, thrust from a sliding jolt from their youthful bodies. *"Pussy-cats"* need not join the game!

The ball got away from time to time, sliding into the rocky raven dividing the grassy field from the ocean waves. They were lucky for this small barrier, with enough space between the playing field and the powerful ocean to allow just a small leeway. There appeared to be some built in pecking order which determined who would retrieve the ball from the raven. Only the boys understood this social system.

The game lasted more than one hour as the evening light gradually faded. The ball took a dive somewhere, and was apparently lost. The older boys left the field, while the young boys stayed behind to search the ravens for the ball. Soon everyone left the field, apparently unable to retrieve their prize.

The next day the small boys returned. I noticed that the ball was found. Someone was persistent enough to search diligently, and it proved successful. Without the interference from the teenagers, this time the young boys could play the game with full participation. They were happy. As the game was over and the sun was setting, they stopped at my veranda to ask for water. I was happy for them.

American Hebrew-Israelite Transitions in Ghana
July 4, 2007

The *Asafohene* **of my village in** *Elmina*, Ghana transitioned Tuesday night, 3 July, 2007 at the hands of a reckless driver, near Dakuma Junction-Accra, Ghana. He was 68 years old. In his United States incarnation in New York he was known at Mr Rob, and was still affectionately known by many locals as *Nana Rob*.

Nana and his wife returned to Elmina with a group of *Afrikan Hebrew Israelites* about seventeen years ago. They so admired the beauty of this ocean side village, and the hospitality of the people, they asked if they could settle in that village. They were graciously granted a large ocean front area, which gradually developed into a unique and beautiful retreat.

Nana Rob will be remembered as one of the pioneers who pushed unceasingly to establish either dual citizenship or permanent resident status for Aboriginal Americans who wished to return to Ghana to live. He was an advocate of Pan African Unity. Ironically, he died on the day and close to the hour that the fifty three nations of the African Union voted in Accra, Ghana to place African Unity on the back burner until an unspecified future time.

When Nana Rob came to Elmina, he never returned to the United States again. He always said that there was no need to return to the USA. He will be buried tomorrow, in the tradition of the Afrikan Hebrew Israelites. The young men in the village dug the grave early this morning in preparation of the body's delivery by sun-down. Because of the official, bureaucratic *"red tape"* the body was not released in time for the burial to take place today in keeping with the traditions of the Hebrew Israelites.

191

Nana Rob, Village Asafohene, Returns Home
10:45 PM--July 4, 2007

The body had just arrived from the capital city of Accra at 8:55 PM. The drums in the village were beating the dirge. The sirens from the undertaker's ambulance were blasting. The young men were ready, standing at the junction of the main highway and Diaspora Road. They were all wearing red and black, the mourning colors. I watched from the front veranda of my oceanfront cottage as the young men followed behind the ambulance to accompany the body to his home, about 500 yards up from the junction. After the sirens stopped, the rain began to pour down again.

I started cooking at 7:30 in the morning after I returned to my cottage with my close Ghanaian lady friends, who knocked on my door before 6:00 AM this morning.

"Is it true what they heard, that Nana Rob is dead?"

"I don't know", I said.

Although I heard the drums all night long, and singing coming from either next door in the village, or two doors down Diaspora Road. I was not sure what it was all about.

Elmina's Bakatue Festival started yesterday, and the men in the cottage in front of my house had been fattening a sheep. I noticed yesterday when I came from the festival that the sheep was no longer tied to the pole near the driveway. So I thought that the sheep was now in the cook pot or over the fire and that the neighbors were eating and celebrating all night long.

I began to make some phone calls. It was news to the brother on the other side down Diaspora Road. He was a new arrival from Atlanta. He is now living In Elmina for about four months. He came with his wife, whose health was deteriorating in the US. They moved to our village for peace and solace.

I called my close informant in the village who confirmed

192

that Nana Rob was killed by a hit and run driver in Accra early yesterday evening. The gong-gong was sounded in the village about 5:00 AM this morning, announcing the sad news.   Nana was on his way to pick up his wife, who was in Accra for the official opening of the *Diaspora House* at the *W.E.B. Dubois Memorial Center.* Nana's car broke down and he was crossing the road to get help. It was dark, with the added danger of *"lights off"* around 7:00 PM, when a white Mercedes nine passenger bus knocked him over and kept going! A *"good Samaritan"* came to his aid, pulled him off the road and flagged down a taxi to take him to the hospital in Accra. He took Nana's phone to call anyone whose number was saved. He did reach friends, who met them at the hospital. Shortly after arriving at the hospital he transitioned.

The rain started as soon as we left the home of the deceased this morning, where we all grieved together and gave our condolences. By the time I wrote my list of food I needed from the market, the rain was pouring down. I knew that I had to find some of the *"comfort food"* for the Aboriginal American community who would surely begin arriving today and tomorrow. Because of the rain the traffic at Cape Coast market was at a standstill. I knew that *Andy's* was the only place where I was sure to get most of the things I needed.

It is 10:30 PM. I delivered food earlier this evening before the body arrived. When a family member told me that 40 guests were expected to accompany the body, I went back home to continue to cook. I sent more food; tomorrow they will need more. Back in the days when I was growing up in the Southern USA, when the ladies heard of a death, they would begin to cook and talk about the dead. Now I understand why.

JAMES BROWN SANCTIFIED
on the Ethiopian New Millennium

It was fitting and proper that on the first day of the new year, the second millennium of the Ethiopian Coptic Calendar, the **Godfather of Soul**, the Honorable James Brown, was sanctified and declared to be *"one of the major Prophets who brought us through the FIRE!!!"* proclaimed Mama Betty, retired Aboriginal American Returnee to Ghana. At the *Feast of the Sabbath* in the African Hebrew Israelite community in Elmina, Ghana, led by a Rabbi, formerly of New York City, we the congregation were fed spiritually and physically to begin the New Year and the new millennium. The irony of this particular day, *Thursday, September 13, 2007*, was that it also coincided with the *first day of Ramadan* and the *first day of the new millennium of the Ethiopian Coptic Calender*, and the Coptic Christian church, which predates the Church of Rome, the Catholics.

For entertainment, the DJ broke out the CD *"James Brown's 50th Anniversary – Live"*. Most of the congregation was over 50 years old, and James Brown took us all back to those days of struggle for change in the 1960's. All of the songs were there!! For the Feast, all the food, the burnt offering of the sacrificial lamb and the bread; the wine was flowing. James Brown reminded us of the those *"good ole bad days"*, when we fought the power, ran for cover and declared our *Pride in being African, Black and Beautiful!!!*

Yes, we were in the heat, we were in the **FIRE**, and it was because of the truth, the joy, the excitement, the reality check, and motivation and the spiritual regeneration and renewal that his music provided for our souls, that we were **BAPTIZED BY FIRE, AND MADE WHOLE**.

There were many, many prophets of those days; the

194

musicians are too numerous to count; Marvin Gay was one, John Coltrane was another. Ironically, Mama Betty Brown wrote in her diary on the morning of the New Year, about our *many prophets that included Martin, Malcolm, Marcus, Elijah, Drew Ali and James Brown.* But James Brown touched all of us, whether we were in Mobile, or San Francisco, DC or Detroit, Cape Coast or Monrovia, New York or Lagos; James Brown reached all of us. His Memory is forever and we will tell our children and our grandchildren, how he molded our lives and brought us strength, courage and pure happiness through his immortal songs.

Brother James Brown, welcome to the ranks of the Sanctified, the Holy, the Immortal Ones. You are most deserving. For the Joy you gave us, you earned this title.

The Fire Next Time

"God gave Noah the rainbow sign; no more water, the Fire next time." So, it was proclaimed by the Honorable James Baldwin, Aboriginal American author and 1960's revolutionary leader, poet, Prophet and Immortal.

I was just a small girl when I read James Baldwin. I almost understood what he was saying, and it resonated deeply within my soul. It is only within recent years that I pulled James Baldwin's words back into my life. One day while I was sitting in my office outside of Atlanta, Georgia, James Baldwin's words took hold of me. I could not rest until I searched the internet to retrieve his words and worlds of wisdom. I was able to pull up the original cover of *"The Fire Next Time;"* I printed the cover and pinned it to my office wall. I knew that, like all moments of inspiration in my life, this moment was leading to something BIG. I didn't know what, but by this time, after all these forty years of preparation and inspiration, I knew that all things would fall into place – at the right time.

In this book, James Baldwin took us through his childhood in Harlem, where his father was a minister in a storefront church. There were less than twenty members at his church, but as the son of a preacher, he was compelled to sit through the services and perform his duties, singing in the choir and collecting the offerings. These offerings were extremely small, but they were a good part of what his father brought home to the table.

At the time that I was reading *"The Fire Next Time"*, the cities of America were literally burning. Yes, *BURNING!!!* In our frustration, and lack of knowledge as to how we could handle Apartheid America, its white patriarchal, elitist attitude and defiance of their unlawful and immoral rule over the peoples of the Earth, we just extinguished all the symbols of their presence. We did this in spite of the fact that this FIRE destroyed our own neighborhoods, our homes, and retail stores. Most of these establishments did not belong to us; hence, by burning them down we were protesting their presence in our communities.

James Baldwin gave us the first **FIRE, the ORIGINAL FIRE,** the **PHYSICAL FIRE** that we used to vent our frustrations. His message was deeper than that. James Baldwin spoke of **the** *Spiritual Fire,* the **FIRE** that lighted the pulpit that his father stood on. The **FIRE** that got the women of Harlem singing and dancing in the isles of that storefront church; the **FIRE** that raised the voices of the church in a resounding beckoning for the *Mother of the Universe* to come down to give them **RESPITE.**

This is the FIRE that we as a PEOPLE are now in POSSESSION OF. WE, the WOMEN of the Aboriginal Diaspora, have asked that the Mother of the UNIVERSE, the *DIVINE MOTHER* who was relegated to the status of *"HOLY SPIRIT"* by the Church of Rome and all the churches' offspring, the Protestants. We have asked that *SHE* intervene on our behalf and *RESTORE and RECAPTURE HER THRONE!!*

In the name of the *HOLY SPIRIT, THE FIRE THAT ROARS WITHIN OUR SOULS, THAT SPIRIT THAT BEGS FOR RELEASE,* so that it can rise to the **HIGHGEST HEAVEN**, to ascend to the height of **SPRITUAL ENLIGHTENMENT,** *THE* **THOUSAND PETAL LOTUS**, we acknowledge this **SPIRIT,** that has been waiting for the last forty years, to bring us to **SALVATION.**

*In memory of the Reverend Dr. Miles Mark Fisher, pastor of the church where I grew up in Durham, North Carolina, I dedicate these words to you, along with the Honorable James Baldwin. Every year at the October anniversary of White Rock Baptist Church, Dr. Miles Mark Fisher preached the "**Ole Time Religion**". It was a beautiful medley of Songs, Hymns and old-fashioned preaching. Choreographed by Mr. John Gaddis,* *musical director of the church, and High School teacher during the 1950's, the choir sang from such a deep level of* **SPIRIT** *that I am to this day, still asking, "Where are the recordings of the "***Ole Time Religion***"? I remember that every year, white folks came to record Dr. Fishers' "***Ole Time Religion***" Month. Where are these recordings???*

One of my favorite songs went like this:

Call:	*I am seeking for a City*
Response:	*Hallelujah*
Call:	*I am seeking for a City*
Response:	*Hallelujah*
Call:	*Oh, a City into the Kingdom*
Response:	*Hallelujah*
Call:	*Oh, a City into the Kingdom*
Response:	*Hallelujah*
Call:	*Children I don't feel no ways tired*

Children, Oh, Glory Hallelujah
And I hope to shout to Glory when this world is on FIRE
Oh, Glory Hallelujah

"God gave Noah the Rainbow Sign, No more Water – The FIRE Next Time". *Thank you, my Immortal Brother,* **James Baldwin.**

Fall Equinox, September 21, 2007 -- Elmina, Ghana – West Africa

199

Party Time—The Water is Here!

Today was interesting, because we ran out of water before 9 AM. I have found a reliable water source now who will fill my poly tank usually the same day, and I don't have to go down to the ocean to fetch sea water to flush my toilet for two days until the water holding tank is filled again.

The weather was extremely hot today. I still had to go the have a mechanic look at the brakes on my car, to see where the noise was coming from. The car repair place resembles certain junk yards in the USA. There are many cars lined up in the dirt lot. The mechanics are an interesting group, all very dirty from car grease, grim and mud, with shirts hanging out and trousers coming down. I sat in a small kiosk pretending to read as I observed the many people, from every walk of life with every type of vehicle, come and go to and from this dirt and grease pit. This is the place where you can get anything repaired on your car for perhaps half the price as any other service station with all the latest sophisticated gadgets and diagnostic tools. These guys could put a car together from scratch within one day, using just a few simple hand tools.

The repairs were small and very reasonable, about 10% of what I would pay for the same service in the USA. I felt good that the brakes were adequate, and that I could continue to ride the bumpy dirt roads safely.

I returned home, exhausted from the heat, to find that the water had not been delivered. I had a small snack, laid down under the fan to cool off, and fell asleep. I don't know how long I slept, but power naps are refreshingly wonderful.

When I awakened, I decided not to fret about the water, so I busied my self with small tasks that I never want to do; I must do them anyway. I kept my hands busy, while I scanned the horizon for any signs of the water tanker truck.

The truck finally arrived, and I began to dash around, to place all available containers near the truck to maximize my total amount of water. I pay for the whole tanker full of water, even though my holding capacity is only half. I collect an addition 50 gallons of water when I fill all my tubs, buckets and containers. So I line them all up.

Before the water tanker begins to fill my tank, a throng of people descend onto my yard. They come with buckets of all sizes and shapes, plastic cans, plastic barrels of all descriptions. It looked like the whole village came to collect a bit of this most precious commodity. After my tank, tubs and containers were filled, some of the village women came to ask if they could please have some of the water. Yes, of course you may share this water!

As the women began to fill their containers, children and young boys all came with 4-6 gallon plastic bottles. Some people were a little over-zealous and brought some very large buckets and tubs to collect water.

There was a great commotion; there was loud talk, arguments, pushing and shoving, but ultimately, everybody collected some water. Those who were a bit greedy soon found out that it is no easy task to carry a 15 gallon barrel of water, so they had to resort to collecting small buckets, a few gallons at a time, and taking them home to the village, just across the open field, maybe 200 yards to the east.

The water truck was emptied. I waved to my friend, the water man, and they drove away. Shortly thereafter, my daughter arrived at the house, having just collected the children from school. She said, *"There's a party going on in the yard!"*

"Yes, everyone is rejoicing because they don't have to walk for 2 kilometers today, in this blazing equatorial sun, with 4 gallons on water on their heads."
Today is a blessed day for a big party!

201

Sleepless With Water

There was no way that I could sleep again at 4:30 AM with water wasting within my earshot. This was my 4th time up since 3:00 AM when I heard the water overflowing from my 1100 gallon water tank. The automatic shut-off valve was long broken by the water company. I filled the bathtub first, then four 5 gallon water cans. The water kept spilling.

Then the rains came. My water holding tank is set up to capture rain water as well; hence another source of water to worry about. Again I stepped out onto the veranda to bring yet another holding vessel inside to be filled. The twenty gallon water bowl was filled; yet the water kept spilling. I couldn't sleep as I thought about the women and children in the village who carry the water on their heads for long distances to attend to their basic household tasks like cooking, bathing and washing clothes. I could not bear the sound of wasting water.

Last year I attempted to help solve the problem of the water shortage within my village. I raised money from friends in the USA to build a water reservoir. I was happy about this accomplishment until I discovered that one of the village leaders used this voluntary contribution as yet another source to extort money from local businesses. To the local business, he claimed that he personally financed the venture, then he collected money from that businesses, then pocketed all that money for himself. I told the village elders about this thievery within their midst. I told them that unless they expose the thief, I could not continue to support the water reservoir project. The thief is still sitting unchallenged in the village.

The water reservoir remains empty. Recently the water company opens the water pipe around 7:00 AM each morning. If you are lazy and don't climb out of bed you loose your chance to fill your water vessels at the communal water pipe in the village. Then the women and children must trek for 2 km to fetch water.

The men sit under the shade tree in front of the water reservoir each day without making a move to either fill the reservoir or to devise a method to capture the rain water or to hook up the communal water line to the reservoir so that water will always be available in the village.

The rain continues to fall, filling my water tank to overflowing. I can't sleep because I can't climb the twenty feet high tower to shut off the water valve; and the most precious resource on earth is simply wasting away.

Wasted Water

I'm glad that I read this email from a girlfriend; I need one now. My only problem is that it is 3:54 AM Greenwich Mean Time and I am in Ghana. There is water flowing, wasting from the poly-tank that was designed to keep me from running out of water. Right now water is running everywhere.

I can't sleep because this valuable resource is going to waste and I can't stop the waste. Last year this time there was no water in this village. I had to buy water about every ten days. Now I have to shut off the water because when I was buying water the municipal water company broke my automatic shut off valve on my poly- tank; somebody has to climb a 25 foot tower to shut off the water. I can't call my assistant at 4:00 AM to climb up the tower to shut off the water. I can't call on a girlfriend to come in the middle of the night to shut off the water. And I can't sleep with water wasting within my hearing.

I guess you can say that I feel a little alone in the world right now. There is no one I can reach out to. Everyone is sleeping, or somehow engaged in their own lives. My water problem is not their concern. I must cheer up and meet many people within the next few hours. I have a scheduled farm visit, where I have invited many people to join me on the farm.

Kwame, my assistant in all my farm endeavors, is suffering from malaria. He came by the house this morning all wrapped up with two long sleeve shirts on and pulled up around his neck. I gave him some malaria medicine and told him to go home to sleep. If he were here he would climb the tower and turn off the water, even at 4:00 AM.

I left the bedroom next to the water tower to escape the sound of water wasting, but I can still hear it, even over the sound of the waves crashing on the coastal rocks just a few feet away from my window.

But my sadness comes not just from the wasting water, but the tortured lives that I see around me. The women and men whom I know, who have shared time with me over the past few days appear to me to be living tortured lives. I really don't know, perhaps I'm reading something that is not there. There seems to be a great deal of victimization, blame, self doubt and usury going on. I know that I have done a lot of baby sitting for grown folks over these past few days. I suppose when you invite people to share in your joys of Africa, you don't realize that they may not be able to enjoy Africa with the open and acceptance way that you enjoy Africa.

The water continues to flow and I wonder if it will stop soon. I don't know how I can sleep as I fall asleep writing this small note to myself.

Please Enjoy this Glass of Water –
With Moringa

It all seemed so simple that it was hard to believe. I personally coined the phase *"When you look for solutions to seemingly insurmountable problems, you find the answers to be quite simple and usually right under your feet."* Therefore, if anyone believes that a glass of water can solve so many of our health concerns, it should be me.

I am surprised that it took me fifteen years to read a book about the miracle workings of simple water. The book, ***"Your Body's Many Cries for Water – Don't Treat Thirst with Medications"***, by F. Batmanghelidj, M.D., was published in 1992 by Global Health Solutions, Inc. This book breaks down into simple terms the physiology of dehydration of the body, and how prolonged dehydration spawns the most common diseases, like diabetes, hypertension, heart disease, asthma and allergies.

Dr. Batmanghelidj, an Iranian born medical doctor, trained at London University's St. Mary's Hospital, received his *"hard knocks"* while his serving sentence in Iran's prison. He was incarcerated after the Iranian revolution of 1979. The prison was a perfect place for clinical trials. Because of the lack of facilities and medications, he was forced to use common sense in treating illness among his fellow inmates. It is in this controlled environment that he discovered that plain water is a potent pain killer.

Americans, who are victims of mass marketing of everything, and especially fast foods and drinks, which only satiate the desire centers of the brain, are generally unaware of how we are psychologically manipulated by radio and television advertising. Madison Ave in New York City, Americas advertising and marketing center, spends billions of dollars each year to create within the populous the thirsts for foods, alcoholic drinks, colas and most recently, the newest pharmaceutical drugs.

Interestingly, the greatest marketing of pills and drugs for every imaginable illness takes place at the close of the work day, when people collapse on their sofas, watching the evening news and attempting to escape the drudgery of another stressful day on the job. They have proven to be the easiest people to persuade, cajole and convince, because of the psychological state of mind that accompanies the stresses of the workplace, almost any workplace in America. Everyone is looking for that little pill that will ease their pain and help them to face tomorrow. The result is a boom in the pharmaceutical industry, with patients asking their doctors for the newest and latest advertised miracle pill. The patients tell their doctors what to prescribe for them!

After his release from prison, he escaped Iran and Dr. Batmanghelidj then relocated to the USA. He has attempted to create an awareness of dehydration as the aetiology, the source, of many diseases. His simple solution water treatment regime has been published in prestigious medical journals and he has lectured at colleges, universities and professional seminars around the world. He contends that the first line of treatment in any disease should be the re-hydration of the body through administering increased water to the patient.

In this book, there are many simple answers to questions about how the lack of water causes stresses in the body. In a dehydrated state, the body then creates conditions that lead to disease. Since the body is made up of 75% water, and only 25% solids, it is common sense that if there is a reduced access to water, the body would automatically go on the defensive. He explains that the intake of other liquids like coffee, tea, juices and sodas are no substitute for water. He also explains how the consumption of these beverages along with alcohol, also *"destroy the natural thirst sensation"*. This is the body's way of telling you that it needs water. Of course, he does not advise that everyone take ten glasses of water each day and throw away the pills. The body does become adjusted to the chemical conditions created by pharmaceutical medicines. These medications often create chemical imbalances which further mask the need for water in the body's healing mechanism. What is advised for most people, except for those with kidney disease, is to begin by slowly adding more water, one or two glasses first thing in the morning and one 8 oz glass one hour before each meal. The increase should take place slowly for three to four weeks. If there is any possibility that you have kidney disease, he advises that you inform your doctor of your desire to try the water treatment approach. If you choose this option, you should also monitor your water intake along with your urine discharge to make sure that there is no excessive retention of water.

Dr. Batmanghelidj also explains the need for salt in the body to maintain homeostasis, or fluid/electrolyte balance. I find it interesting that most hypertension and heart patients are placed on a low salt diet along with diuretics, which further dehydrates and weakens the body, hence creating further disease states. Another condition that results from dehydration is the amino acid, or protein imbalance. This imbalance produces immune disorders which then result in conditions which are tagged as HIV and auto-immune diseases, such as arthritis and lupus, where the body begins to consume itself because of the lack of water and essential amino acids to the cells.

The solutions are simple, more **Clean water** and **Moringa oleifera**, a complete vegetable protein, which also contains naturally occurring zinc and selenium. Dr. Batmanghelidj recommends all vegetable sources of proteins along with zinc to bring about the balance in the body which will allow natural healing to take place. All of these are necessary for the body to revert to its normal state. According to research conducted by the National Institutes of Health in Bethesda Maryland, **Moringa oleifera**, also known as *Nebedaye*, is the richest, most nutrient dense vegetable source of multivitamins and minerals every created. These are 100% bio-available nutrients in the plant. Neither Madison Avenue or the pharmaceutical industry or the American Medical Association will tell you how simple it is to restore your health. Here it is *Coyote Creek Aquifer Water* and *Moringa Power Plus*. Try it for a better life.

Coyote Creek Aquifer Water is the brand name for the Artesian Water from a local well in Georgia. For more information contact:
Herbaful Nutrients: *Atlanta, Georgia USA at*
www.herbaful.com

404 767-4786.

The Five Tastes of Moringa Seeds
Farm Report – May 21, 2008

Kwame and Ali spent the afternoon cracking the hulls from the Moringa seeds. It was tedious work, but we thought that we would give it a try to do a little relaxing after working so hard planting Moringa cuttings on the farm today. Removing the seed hulls is so tedious we decided to give the job to some school girls at the farm tomorrow. They would be happy to make a little cash during their vacation time.

At the day's closing I asked the guys if they tasted the seed. They said no. I told them that in Thailand the people are now using the seeds to treat HIV/AIDS. They chew three seeds daily. Both guys grabbed a few seeds and began to chew. Kwame immediately said, *"This seed tastes hot, sweet, bitter and salty, and when it goes down it tastes like nuts."*

Immediately I remembered by training in **Traditional Oriental Medicine** and how *Differential Diagnosis* uses the five tastes to access the body's dysfunctions. ***I told Kwame that he has innocently pointed out why the seeds of the Moringa tree have such distinctive healing properties.*** Like the leaves which contain almost every vitamin and mineral needed to maximize the human body's metabolic interactions, the seeds contain the ingredients needed to nourish the organs to enhance the body's optimal functioning.

The five tastes are associated with specific organs; stomach/spleen=sweet, kidney /bladder = salty; liver/gall bladder= sour; lungs /large intestines = hot/spicy; heart /small intestines = bitter.

No Redress

Is this Nkrumah's Vision of Ghana?

Letter to the Chairman of the CPP – Nkrumah's Party

Dear Sir:

I address a topic that every passenger and driver in Ghana is aware of. No one seems to be able to control it. I speak to you because you have been given the task to carry forth the legacy and vision of our great leader, Osagyefo Dr. Kwame Nkrumah.

Yesterday, Sunday afternoon, 17 June, 2007, a driver who was illegally overtaking to pass three cars from behind me crashed into my car, tearing the front fender and light. I was turning left into a petrol station, my turn signal was flashing. Many witnesses saw, and all agreed that the driver who hit my car was at fault. The witnesses begged me to report to the police, but then on second thought advised me that the police would only ask for money, and the driver would not pay for the damage.

Nyame adom, by God's Grace I was not injured. Had my car turned only one meter more to the left, I would not be alive and sitting here today. When police corruption is so acute that everyone knows that you cannot go to them with a legitimate complaint, something must change. Otherwise, our beloved Ghana will deteriorate into a lawless society of foraging goats and sheep, all looking for the next opportunity to *"chop"*. Osagyefo is turning in his grave.

Please see attached description I wrote after the accident.

Kali Sichen

Sunday, 17 June, 2007

It was about 5:05 PM when a car, passing illegally in front of the Shell Station in Elmina, swooped passed me and tore off the fender and the signal/parking lights of the car. The car was not severely damaged, and I was not hurt at all, just shaken a lot.

I calmly drove into the Shell station, made my purchase at the convenience store, calmly went back out to secure the drivers' and the cars' particulars. I knew that if I went to the police station, I would only create problems for myself. First there would be a bribe that I would have to pay, and if I wasn't careful, I might be arrested, even though the fault was not mine. All the witnesses at the Shell station saw what happened and knew that the driver was totally at fault. I have no redress. The police would see only $$$$.

Sometimes I believe that certain people join the Ghana police force in order to secure their daily *"chop money"* or *"bribe"* from motorists who, for whatever reason, would rather pay the *chop money* than to go through the long hassle of dealing with the police, the courts or any other government agency.

Because there is corruption at every level in government with malfunctions throughout, government agents, be it from the small town police station all the way up to the immigration officer, are undisciplined. This makes doing the right thing difficult, because if you want to move forward in this society, you may have trouble finding anyone who will help you to do the right thing. Too many officials want to get paid, under the table, for what they are supposed to do according to their job description.

Hence, I sit here with a broken fender and a broken headlight. I was just a split second from losing my life from a car illegally passing three cars on a two lane highway in a heavily traveled area, with many cars and many people on foot inside the town of Elmina, Ghana.

God is good, because just one split second later, I might have been killed along with many others in the many cars as well as innocent bystanders. *"Nyame adom"*, by God's Grace, I am alive, and I can write about this. I have no redress within this government, the insurance company or the police and motor vehicle department. But the Great Spirit spared my life and many others today, and I am most grateful.

One hour later, I sit at my computer to tell the world what happened. *Nyame Adom!! By God's Grace!!*

This just a Report. This is not to say that, in many cases in America, many Aboriginal-Indigenous people, called African Americans, are in the same boat -- No Redress - from the corrupt and dangerously lethal police, the corrupt insurance companies and the government services corporations.

6:03PM

Trashing Paradise -- Part I

"Mommy, that man just boo-boo," the three year old girl shouted as she ate breakfast on the veranda of our cottage on Diaspora Road.

The small girl born in America could not believe that she witnessed a grown man lower his pants to defecate on the beach just below our cottage in this small fishing village. I must admit that she was far more observant than I. I have seen the men pass by my window in the early morning hours, but I did not follow their action to see what they were doing. Just this morning I noticed one of the men kneel between the coastal rocks, then to rise shortly thereafter pulling up his pants. From the mouth of babes comes the truth.

One of the habits I have observed that deeply disturbs me is the rampant, unrestrained urination and defecation in public places. Certainly, in the old days when the villages were surrounded by forests, such behavior was commonplace and expected. Today in these urban settings, facilities must be made to address these sanitation issues.

The Members of Parliament, District Assemblymen and local administrators should make sanitation and water the prime issue to address the needs of the people. From what I have observed, the primary health concern, instead of being AIDS or malaria, should be the poor sanitation conditions. Certainly, malaria is a big concern, and everyone to whom I speak about their health condition reports that they are suffering from malaria. Is it really malaria, or is it a bacterial or viral condition resulting from environmental contamination due to public defection and urination, with the resulting illnesses which arise from fecal/e-coli contamination?

I am not criticizing, I am only commenting on an observation. When I spoke to my daughter about the practice of

214

using the beach as a toilet, she reminded me that in the USA and every other developed nations, sewage is also released into the rivers, creeks and oceans, so all fecal materials in all parts of the world are destined to find their way to the oceans. Hence, since time began, the ocean has absorbed everybody's body wastes. The foreigner's problem with seeing the public display of defecation and urination is that in the developed world, this practice is hidden from public view. In the western world there are small rooms called toilets where people go to release their body wastes in private, and it all still ends up in the--oceans.

There are things that men can do for themselves. I have seen some of the same men passing my window early mornings, sitting under the shade tree all day long. Apparently, they have no work and nothing to do with their time. I ask where are the pioneers, the innovators the motivators who can turn this human resource into a progressive workforce? Who can step forward to lead these men into a place of dignity and self respect? I know that these men don't want to idle their time away every day. Where is the leadership to step forward to give them the boost they need to move out of this stagnation?

On this the 50th anniversary of Ghana's independence, there must be a progressive voice somewhere that can remind the people of their heritage. To remember *Osagyefo Dr. Kwame Nkrumah* without attempting to renew his vision and to re-implement his plans for Ghana's truly independent future would be a travesty to his memory. I challenge the government of Ghana, and especially the local government officials who administer over this profitable tourist region, to step out of their comfort zone of self interest to move toward community development, especially with water and sanitation.

I challenge all of the preachers who scream at the people from the radio and on to the street corners and church podiums, announcing that *"cleanliness is next to godliness,"* to actually take the proceeds from the Sunday morning collection plate to install bath and toilet facilities in the communities they minister to. I also challenge the preachers in America, whom I have personally heard brag about the churches and clinics that they have built, or are building in Africa, to take the first step to build toilet and bath facilities, before they build any grand *"house of worship"*.

This past summer a friend who was traveling through Ghana with a missionary group, told me that when she asked to use the toilet at the church where she was visiting. This caused quite a stir because there was no toilet at the church! The people were embarrassed and one member offered to drive the lady to her home where the visitor could relieve herself. So I beg my fellow Aboriginal Americans to encourage the building of a church and a clinic around bath and toilet facilities. The physical health of the people must accompany the spiritual health; otherwise, your missionary work has come to naught. There will be no healthy person around to hear your sermons!

Returning to the issue of my surrounding village, and I say mine, because I feel at home here on Diaspora Road. I have adopted this village, with all of its beauty and its challenges. There is simply no excuse why the taxes being collected at the many resort hotels in this town can not be used to provide the local people with collective toilet and bath facilities!

The self-serving attitude of the African governments can not move forward into this twenty fist century in the mode of today's *"quasi democracies"*. A true democracy, government *"by the people and for the people"* does not mean that those who represent the people are the sole beneficiaries of the country's goods and services. This does not happen in Europe, America or Japan. The people may not benefit as much as the top echelon, but they do have minimal sanitary facilities. The African democracies or should I say, autocratic states, should provide minimal services to all their constituents. They especially lack the absolute basics like water and sewer services.

I recently learned that some residential homes built within the last few years do not always provide toilet facilities. I watched as one house was being built just last year. There were about four one room apartment chambers, and a separate kitchen facility to be shared by all. I casually asked a neighbor if she knew of any rental property available, and she pointed to this new building. When I inquired of the availability of the rooms I was told that there was no toilet. I wondered how in 2006, a residential building could be constructed legally without having a toilet? I was told that an outhouse was built but because of the foul odor being carried by the ocean breeze, the outhouse was abandoned. Let me inform you that this building was just 200 yards away from a small resort hotel, and about 500 yards away from a major beach resort hotel! How can an inadequate building be constructed legally, and rented out, in a location so close to a major tourist-area?

In small villages such as this one where I live, simple sewage disposal facilities can be built by the inhabitants for very little money. The men who are sitting around all day, can simply dig septic tanks with adequate drainage lines to provide toilet facilities. A water well can be dug right here near the beach to provide a constant water source to supply the toilets even if the well water is salty. However, I know of a coastal rest stop just 15 miles from here that uses well water for everything. The water from that well is not salty. I suggest that my village begin this process; just try, just try! Osagyefo Dr. Kwame Nkrumah's spirit is crying for Ghana. *"Forward - Ever—Backwards - Never!!!"*

217

Trashing Paradise - Part II

I remember the old days when Ghana cities, towns and villages were pristine, beautiful, uncontaminated. This was before the great onslaught and invasion of plastic packaging, plastic wrapping and plastic bags. I remember the old days when food was wrapped almost exclusively in leaf or paper, with newspaper being one of the most popular wrappings. I remember how, when these wrappings were discarded, the ever present neighborhood goats would come along and consume these wrappings.

Over the past few years since the bagging of drinking water there seems to be so much plastic, which is popularly known in Ghana as *"rubber"*. This carelessly tossed debris makes the roads, market places and the whole of Ghana like a wasteland of disposed, trampled plastic rubbish. In cities and towns it is so bad now that the once clear and open sewers are so chocked with plastic refuse that nothing passes through these gutters during the heavy downpour of rain. Trash continues to pile up.

Providing clean, clear drinking water at a reasonable price for public consumption addresses one of the greatest health issues in Africa. I am happy for this innovation of bagged water. However, the problem of the disposal of the plastic bags must also be a part of the solution; otherwise addressing one health issue only creates another health hazard. It remains to be seen which contamination is the greatest threat, clean drinking water verses clogged sewage drains that result in environmental pollution and improper or inadequate disposal of waste and sewage waters.

I hear many complaints about illness here in Ghana, and malaria is blamed for most illnesses. I believe that the overwhelming abundance of trash mostly resulting from plastic waste and the environmental hazards that improper disposal of sewage water leads to, is just as much to blame for illness as the malarial mosquito. Bad water causes just as much illness; therefore,

218

we can not throw away the bagged water. We must solve the problem of plastic disposal.

I see that this issue is addressed often and in many forums. Trash disposal and the importance of a clean environment are taught in all the school books, beginning at the kindergarten, at a very early age. However, there appear to be few, if any dust bins (*garbage cans*) provided on public streets, school yards, and class rooms or even in village compounds.

I understand that, before I came to Ghana for this extended stay, a government official began a campaign to encourage the people to patrol themselves in trashing the streets. Because of his television and radio ads, it became popular for Ghanaian citizens to remind each other not to throw trash on the streets-without-regard.

Something happened to stop this progressive movement. Somehow, it was discovered that the vice president had a big house in London. Now, this man was a wealthy man before he rose to this political position. Having a house in many capitals of the world is not unusual for the wealthy and privileged. Yet, this piece of news was used as leverage to discourage the environmental clean-up movement that he started. So I wonder who was behind this *"leak"* which caused a scandal that led to discontinuing his *"anti-trash movement."* Whoever it was, their motive had to be to keep the people down, with their heads bowed, discouraged and disenchanted, so that they would disregard the dirt in their environment and the garbage in their sewers.

My household trash disposal became an issue when I found out that the trash that I was giving to my young helpers to dispose of was finding its way into the sea. Perhaps I misunderstood the youth when they said there was a dumpster in their village. Consequently,and without my knowledge, my household trash was left at the seashore for the waves to wash-away.

I was abhorred when I discovered this, when a village elder

advised my helpers, in my presence, to simply through the rubbish into the sea. Hence, all the teachings about environmental cleanliness in the schools come to naught when the elders disrespect their own back yards and the sea that provides them with much of their daily diet. There appears to be a dis-connect in the understanding between environmental and water pollution and a safe and healthy seafood supply.

There is a notable parallel and comparison between environmental pollution that I witness here in Africa, and the environmental degradation in the Aboriginal ghettos of America. I believe that much of this disrespect for one's own environment is rooted in a lack of love for self and little self respect. Hence, as a result of this self-abnegation there is a disregard for one's own environment because the people do not believe that they deserve anything-better.

Of course, we can all point to the historical reasons that brought about this attitudinal behavior on both sides of the Atlantic, i.e., colonialism, slavery and white supremacy indoctrination, with each of these social traditions using the most potent of weapons – religion.

Aside from these factors, there are the political institutions that contribute to these dynamics. When there are no trash cans provided in public places, there is no way to discard rubbish. When there is no regular municipal street cleaning provided, the rubbish continues to pile up. It has always been my contention that the social institutions, both church and state, work hand in hand to deliberately demoralize the people, thus making them feel as if they don't deserve a better environment or better living conditions. After all, according to their Bible teachings, Aboriginal people are the sons and daughters of Ham, the "cursed one." **This is not true at all!**

So here we stand today, having successfully diagnosed our diseased state of mind. We understand the roots of our behavior, yet we appear to be unable to grab hold of these dis-functions and turn things around for our own betterment. Most of us point to the government as the party responsible for not cleaning up our environment. Few of us, however, on either side of the Atlantic Ocean, will admit that much of the responsibility for our self-abnegation lies in the religious indoctrination fed to us from infancy to old age. In fact, we defend the church with more vehemence than we defend our own families.

We have to take responsibility for breaking these shackles of mental enslavement. No one will change our environment, clean up our streets and gutters, our waterways and our villages and neighborhoods except us. We must understand the politics of open sewers, trash on the roadways, no garbage disposal system. These inadequacies, environmental wastes and filth, are designed to keep you from rising up to your highest potential and aspirations. If you don't respect yourself, you don't respect your neighbor and you don't believe that either of you-deserve-better.

If our political leaders are not encouraging us to break these psychological chains that keep us from progressing, we need to change our politics. If our religious leaders are not charging us to work in our villages and neighborhoods to improve the environment, we need to leave our Sunday morning moaning sessions to gather our neighbors to clean up the rubbish at our front doors and on the steps of our churches. Our lives are at stake, because our health is directly related to the state of our environment. Until we get this into our thick skulls, our chances for progress are imperiled.

Today was Like San Francisco

Today I had a little bit of nostalgia; not too much however. I settled some unfinished business in Cape Coast, and then went to the market to buy some things to make potato salad and a birthday cake. It is unbelievable what you pay for ingredients for good ole potato salad like my Mama used in make in North Carolina. These ingredients are not common but they are available at specific shops in the main shopping hub. Really, they cost no more than what I would pay in the USA, but in Ghana, that's a lot of money!

Before I left the market there was a big cloud looming, headed straight at us from the nearby rain forest preserve, Kakum National Forest. It rains a lot there at Kakum about 20 miles north, but sometimes we don't even see a drop of water here on the coast. This cloud looked like it would make it here so I had my assistant drop me at the cottage while he continued to the Elmina market to pick up some things just altered by the seamstress. I wanted to watch the lightning over the ocean, and hear the thunder clap, all while safely tucked away and sheltered on the screened veranda. What a life!

The rain did indeed come. It was short and sweet and by Ghana standards this was not real rain. It cooled the air nicely and to my delight and amazement, the clouds remained low over the ocean and the day looked like twilight at 2:30 in the afternoon.

The mist lay heavy over the ocean at Elmina. I remembered the hundreds of days that I walked the beaches of San Francisco, on the Pacific Ocean where the mist met the ocean waters and lay there like a blanket all day long. The weather would keep cool, and even in the hottest of summer, the temperature at the beach never increased above 65ºF. What a life!

It was for this reason that I loved San Francisco -- 65ºF in summer, and for the same protection from the fog, never less than 45ºF in the winter. I lived in San Francisco for almost my entire

222

adult life, more than 32 years, and there was only one freeze. It killed all of my beautiful *Agave americana* and so many other tropical plants that thrive in San Francisco.

I was a little disappointed that the lightning show was so short over the Atlantic Ocean this afternoon. The coolness dismissed my state of mind, and I enjoyed watching the young boys from the village sitting on top of the huge rock that bulges from the sea like a women's bosom. The boys had a small fishing line. I was afraid for them because the waves were waging war against the rocks and it looked like a big wave would claim them as fodder for the sea.

But the boys sat cool, calm, content and motionless. Then suddenly I saw the two boys pulling vigorously on the fishing line – no fishing pole, you see. These boys were fishing for dinner. This was not a sport! Both of them pulled and pulled; another boy saw them pulling so he joined them. There is nothing like getting in on the tail end to enjoy the fruits of the labor. The prize appeared. I could see it plainly from the distance, so it was a sizable catch.

I thought about San Francisco. I never really saw many people fishing on the Pacific Ocean side. Long years ago when there was a jetty that jutted out from the beach I used to see a lone fisherman every now and then, usually someone of Asian descent. Sometimes I would see some ambitious ones who would dig in the sand for the Abalone. I used to ask for the shells, but no one ever sold me any.

What about the hungry people in San Francisco, I asked myself? Would they take a fishing line and spend the day waiting patiently for a bite from a BIG ONE? Something told me quietly that the answer is NO! Those hungry ones are standing in line at the **Salvation Army** doorstep in downtown San Francisco. Others are standing in the line at the **Glide Memorial Church** in the *Tenderloin* district, waiting for a hot meal! They would be lucky to

223

be served fresh fish. If they get any fish at all, it would probably be imported from China. However, the fish would probably be harvested and processed on a Chinese fishing trawler some 14 miles off the coast of San Francisco and sold to a distributor in Chinatown. What a life! What a world!

I still miss San Francisco. But I look forward to the days of this rainy season on the Coast of Africa in Ghana, at Elmina, where I listen to the roar of the thunder, watch the lightning show over the Atlantic Ocean and smell the fresh breeze from the Antarctic, where nothing but ocean lies between me and the South Pole.

Life was too Hard for Mr. Cobbina

Today we began the great harvest of the Moringa leaf on the farm at Nsanfo-Anomabo, Ghana which were planted last November, 2006. My partner and I went to the farm with the house staff and my god-son, 16 year old Willie. There were four local farmers working with us today.

By 1:00 PM, the sun had beaten us so badly, and we had harvested more leaf than we could process today, so we drove back to Elmina to begin the next phase. We were all sitting together on the ocean side veranda working with the Moringa leaf when a village elder came to tell us that Billie's father died at noon today. None of us were shocked by the news, because my dear friend, Mr. Cobbina, teacher and African historian had been very ill for a many months.

Mr. Cobbina wanted to die; he willed his death. I think that it took him longer than he expected. What he suffered from was a mystery; he faded away. It was the same illness that his brother suffered from just three years ago; he faded away, and left a nine year old son, Mick, to his brother, Cobbina. Cobbina rejected all the help, suggestions and assistance that I offered to him to help him to regain his health and strength.

Life was too hard for Cobbina. When his mother died several years ago he borrowed money from the bank to pay for her funeral. His monthly paycheck from the Junior Secondary School where he taught, went straight to the bank. After the bank took its share, there was not enough money to care for his family, and he was especially saddened that the school fees for all the children exceed his monthly salary. He worked hard on his orange grove last summer. The work was too much, and he couldn't afford to hire help. His eldest child, beautiful Efua, nineteen years old, starts nurse's training school in September.

Tomorrow is another farm day, and we must complete the harvesting. Five young girls from Nsanfo village, ages fifteen years and sixteen years, will join us in the harvesting. I am happy for their assistance, because this phase of the work is labor intensive and tedious.

Billie will not join us tomorrow. About 2 hours ago his mother arrived from another village in the heart of the cocoa growing region of Ghana where she is the ruling Queen Mother. She will sit with Cobbina's present wife and widow, Adom, until tomorrow when all the local family will gather together to begin planning for the official burial rites and the long ceremonies surrounding Ghana funerals.

Life was too hard for Cobbina. He took the easy way out. God bless you, Cobbina, and I know that you will continue to teach West African history, now that you have joined the ancestors.

I Pray that the Lights Don't Go Off

Electricity is becoming a very rare commodity in Ghana these days, especially now at the end of the dry season. Almost all the power in Ghana comes from the damn at Akosombo; it is generated solely by the water from the Volta River. The river is very low at the end of the dry season; hence, we have experienced more and more frequent *"lights off"*. Even after the rainy season last year, everyone had *"lights off"* at least once a week. Over the past two weeks, we have had *"lights off"* every other night.

For a busy person like me, who goes to the farm at least twice a week, and certainly every morning after a rain, my days are filled, and I seldom have the time to write or to look at my email during the day. Therefore, I pray that there is electricity so that I can do some work at night.

Over the past six months, while living in this cottage with my daughter and four grandchildren, 22 months, 3 years, 6 years and 8 years old, I sat on my veranda at night, in total darkness, watching the waves in the Atlantic ocean, the moonlit sky, and the lights on the fishing trawlers far out at sea. I sat for hours, while my daughter bathed the children and set them to bed. The house would quiet, and I would continue to sit in the dark. In fact, I have refused to install a light bulb on the ocean side veranda, because of the peace, quiet and comfort of the darkness.

My night time visitors, who are rare, know that they will sit in the dark with me, because that is what I do each night. The kerosene lanterns are used only in the bathroom. We have no need for them in other places in the house while lights are out. We simply go to sleep, or sit in the dark.

I grieved for a short time for the family moving away. It is a good move for everyone, especially for my daughter, who really needed to get away from her children sometimes. In her new house now she has her own room, and no longer has to share her bed with one or children. This is a good break for her.

Yes, I pray that the lights don't go out before I send this email, because I just don't want to loose my thoughts and have to write this note again.

Today is my birthday, and I had a very exciting time. We brought 300 pieces of bamboo, 3" in diameter and 8ft-6in long, from the village near my farm. The truck we used was the *"push-to-start"* type. About 10 boys 14-19 years, who are members of our **G.E.N.E.S.I.S.** team, along with 3 adult leaders, got the truck started outside my cottage and it chugged along on the 18 mile journey to the bamboo site. It was quite an ordeal to push start the truck after it was filled with bamboo, so five village men joined the team to push start the truck to return to Iture-Elmina.

We are building spectator benches for the football field and a shelter for the bonsai plants, all a part of the G.E.N.E.S.I.S. Project. Tomorrow we begin another project to build a taxi and transportation shelter at the roadside next to the village, another G.E.N.E.S.I.S. Project.

We arrived just as night fell; we were happy that there were lights, because it would have been difficult to unload all that bamboo in total darkness. *"Lights off"* means *"no fans"*, and that makes for a very tough time, when you have a prickly heat rash.

Independent Communities

My Dear Brother,

I hope that all is well with your family and with your most important mission in Atlanta, the **Akoben Institute**. Recently I was studying your DVD on *Warriorhood*, as I clearly see the *"handwriting on the wall"* showing us that self reliance and self sufficiency within independent communities-nation states (complete with army), is truly the path that the USA is headed. Those of us who do not heed the ***"handwriting on the wall"*** and do not make preparations for their own survival will be left outside of those walls. It will be somewhat like the doors closing on "**Noah's Ark**".

Several weeks ago a *"blueprint"* for forming independent communities was floating around the internet. I received the email from many friends, from Atlanta to California to Nigeria. When our mutual friend in Nigeria saw the *"blueprint"* she sent an email to both/all of us saying that *"we need to talk to each other."* This is because she knows that we have already developed a large plot of land in Ghana that is food and shelter independent and we are well on our way to energy independence at our 22 acre *Global Model Forest for Self Sufficiency*. I was very busy at that time and engaged in some activities that kept me from following through. The *"handwriting"* is clearer by the day, and we need to look very seriously at making some moves as a collective.

About five years ago when we first introduced the **G.E.N.E.S.I.S. Project** (*Growing Energy and Nutrition for Environmental Stability & Investments in our Societies*) there was only a vague interest. Because we could not drum up the necessary support, almost three years ago we began the journey alone. I have been the point person on the ground in Ghana during this development stage.

Tropical Africa is a wonderful place to show how quickly one can become nutritionally independent because crops grow very fast. We have and endless summer here. Having this project well on the way to stabilizing here in Ghana is very satisfying; many people say, however, that most of our people in the Diaspora in the Americas will never consider settling in Africa, and that we need to establish a similar project somewhere in America. I agree.

This **Model Forest** was always meant to be a *"Model"* that could be duplicated anywhere and everywhere that Aboriginal people live, be it on the continent or somewhere in the various nations in North and South America or the islands in the Pacific and Indian Oceans. Aboriginal people are everywhere, as our brother Runoko Rashidi has clearly shown us. As a people one of our greatest fortunes is that most of the lands that the Great Spirit has blessed us with is tropical and we have the distinct advantage of rain and sunshine to grow many crops each year. (I *am attaching a letter from one of our sisters in the Afrikan Diaspora in Europe who clearly shows us that our people in Europe do not share the same good fortune for survival and self sufficiency because they lack the land and the weather that would allow their independence!)*

Just how we can convince our people that they need to look at food and energy independence is a mystery to me. We have been talking about this since 1995; now thirteen years later there are still only a few *"believers"*. And now that our people foolishly believe that the *"Messiah"* has come in the cloak of **Barak Obama**, perhaps most are still not willing to listen. But even the so-called *"Messiah"* says that we must help ourselves!

North Scale Education and Research Institute in Georgia

Independent Communities
Plan B – Update

"The words of the Prophets are written on the subway walls and tenement halls."
"The Sound of Silence" (Simon & Garfunkel, 1960's)

I have been an optimist all of my life; as I grow older and perhaps a little wiser, I have become more practical. I see things as they are, even as I am wishing and hoping for the best case scenario to unfold.

This initiation into mature and practical reality came about when a prophecy was painted and written on the Ocean Beach Break-Wave wall at the Pacific Ocean in San Francisco, California; the wall is 20 feet high at its highest point and descends to about 10 feet tall along a two – three mile stretch of oceanfront. The paintings started appearing in early 1995, sometime around February. As a daily exercise, my partner and I used to walk on the beach every morning; it was about a 3 mile trek. One day there appeared some mysterious symbols about 15-20 feet tall that drew us to the beach wall. As a life-long student of symbols and symbolism, I knew that there was a deep meaning and a grand story was taking shape. Over the next two years we religiously recorded with video and photography the emerging story which we called *"The Cosmic Prophecies of San Francisco"*. Below are some of the major events that were prophesied

- The Bush Family White House Dynasty
- Never ending World War
- Wasted and squander financial resources belonging to the people of America
- Uncontrolled greed and avarice of a few wealthy at the top of the economic strata

231

- Moral decay in the form of sex, drugs, gambling and alcohol
- 9-11, the fall of great buildings
- Mass Mind Control through media domination of the power elite
- Healing Herbs that would save the people (Moringa)
- Alien invasion

All of the events predicted in *"The Cosmic Prophecies of San Francisco"* have come to pass except perhaps the Alien invasion (maybe). For the next two years, 1995-1997 my partner and I traveled the length and breadth of the USA, from Coast to Coast, North to South, East to West and circling America at least 10 times, showing a slide show of the wall paintings and warning the people of the times to come.

Today (September 25, 2008) my 87 year old sister (same mama & daddy) voiced her concern over the looming financial crisis of the company holding her retired teacher's fund and apparently nearly all the retirement funds for the teachers in the whole of America. She told me about the shortage of gasoline and the closing of the biggest car dealership in Atlanta, Georgia. This is a tremendous economic blow to Atlanta. My sister even whispered the word "soup lines". She actually saw these things before, because she lived through the Great Depression. I reminded you all that back in the days of the Great Depression most of us had family members who were still farming. Those days of food security are gone.

On June 12, 2008 I wrote the following message to my internet friends and partners. I send the below document to you again, as I see emerging what also appears to be another prophecy. We must take our heads out of the sand and begin to make plans for an uncertain future.

This is not pessimism – this is realism!!!

232

Independent Communities
Plan C – A Must

Aboriginal Americans are all jubilating over the possibility that we could see our very first Black President in the United States (in recent years; John Hanson, a Moor, preceded George Washington). Our sister Alice Walker in her email letter of March 21, 2008 reminded us that, even if Obama wins the election and we have a Black President, First Lady and First Family, he will inherit so many problems of such a great magnitude that it will take *"Divine Intervention"* to straighten things out. If elected and he gets past the first 100 days, any major tasks accomplished will be a miracle.

Look at the issues Obama would have to deal with **BEFORE** he begins to consider the problems of race and the continuing *"white privilege"* at the root of American societal dysfunction:

1. War in Iraq; how will the military industry like their *sugar-baby* taken away from them?
2. Wounded and maimed soldiers, over 20,000 who must be cared for
3. Mortgage crisis – who will save your homes? Will the banks be saved first?
4. Where will the people live when their homes are taken away and there are no jobs?
5. Financial (American dollar) Instability – The dollar is falling so fast we don't know if it will buy anything by inauguration day. America owes money to China mostly; Chinese goods are upholding the dollar, but when will China ask for re-payment? Will it be shortly after the Olympics, or will the dollar hold up that long?

6. Energy Crisis – How will you get to work (if you still have a job) when the gasoline is too expensive and/or your car is repossessed?

For all of the above reasons we Aboriginal Americans better start looking for a PLAN. In the old days, during the Great Depression (1929 – 1939) we still had relatives on the farms in the South. We had access to food from our relatives in those days, but what do we have now? Now most of those farms are gone, and we are again a land-less people. We own less land now than we did during the Depression days.

Most of us have abandoned the knowledge and skill of providing for our own basic needs. Booker T. Washington told us that we needed to know how to grow food, build houses and provide housing infra-structure (plumbing and electricity) and make clothing. Very few of us have any of these survival skills now Don't bury your head in the sand thinking that all we need is a Black President and everything will be all right. We Aboriginals in the Diaspora have behaved as *"hunter-gatherers"* since we lost our skills of self-sufficiency and survival. We think only about what we need today, and we make no plans for tomorrow. We are still reeling from hurricane Katrina, and waiting for somebody else to provide for our basic needs. Is this not the ***"slave mentality?" "Massa gon' take care o' us." Massa gon'*** take care of himself and his family first! So we had better look at Plan C.

Elmina, Ghana

Farm Photos - Community Helpers
Seize the Moment

An Afro-European Speaks

I know it is not relevant to the current U.S. situation learning survival techniques and sustainability when it comes to the organization for survival. You are lucky! This is for your daughters and all the other brothers and sisters on the other side of the Atlantic:

"The country you were born in the U.S. of A. is rich, really rich. It is vast, has extensive resources and very fertile earth. We learned it in geography the U.S. has black earth, the most fertile of all! You could harvest crops 3 times a year. I - on the other hand - live in a country that depends on the goodwill of its trading partners, since we cannot even feed ourselves.

We do not have enough land or space. Everything is expensive. Land or houses only really rich people can buy. No middle class person can afford a house here. If a critical mass of Aboriginal-Americans would focus for mental/financial self-determination this crisis could be an opportunity.

Many of you still have land, land means freedom! I don't have to tell you, you know much better than me. I am building up a business with a Liberian friend between Switzerland and Africa, because this is what I am forced to do. After almost 20 years of hard work I have not been able to save anything because this place is so expensive. Even when I was working for the corporate world I could never afford a house, let alone land. Up to this day money cannot impress me, no matter how much, because I have grown up during a wealthy period here. But show me land, even a spot, and I will always be impressed. YOU HAVE LAND IN THE U.S. IF IT GETS REALLY BAD - WE CANNOT EVEN GROW OUR OWN FOOD HERE!

Isn't there a way to create self-sufficient places like yours in Ghana in the U.S. for Black youth and adults? I am being very idealistic here, but one has to look at all possibilities. You have so much land, even oil.

I remember the first time I landed in Washington D.C. I immediately understood what the first Europeans must have felt when

237

they landed. They were poverty-stricken, illiterate, disease-inflicted, religiously oppressed and distorted humanity over centuries coming from a continent that is already old, tired and overworked in agriculture. The energy of the earth in the USA was overwhelming.

I've only been to Chicago, Washington D.C. and Baltimore but the aura of the U.S. I will never forget. The first Europeans must have been drooling when they saw the lush nature and nearly untouched wealth and bigness of the place. When I came back to Europe, I tried to tell Euro-Americans about my experience and to my amazement they did not understand what I meant. When I said, "Your country has a strong aura, the energy is very, very strong, a rich country in spirit, not just big with oil etc," they simply looked at me and shook their heads.

This is not the 50s, 60s or 70s anymore. Thank God. We have a real opportunity - the biggest since 500 years to create something new out of this crisis. This crisis is a real opportunity for people to start rethinking their positions and what is really important in life. Not competition - but solidarity.

The U.S., I think is now 50%, 50% right? 50% white, 50% non-whites? White people are getting weaker in opposing us. I see the KKK-I see them - they are so small in their head, so ugly and limited I almost feel for them - only almost - I can never forget what they have done and the pain they continue to inflict to my brothers and sisters who have struggled successfully for so long to inspire Black movements all over the world.

However, I have a feeling that many do not realize that or value it. Only money seems to count. We need more Black international networking, especially now that Africa is growing, now that the white world seems to crumble. Now is a huge opportunity. But if there is no knowledge of what is happening on the other side of the border then how can we network? I am not talking about the minority who knows anyway. I am talking about the masses

I'm not the first to think like this, I know; this situation is unique – and opportunities need to be seized!"
Carole

238

My Response:

You are not babbling, my Sis. You are talking more sense than most that I know. I will share your words with the many because you are coming from the place that so many look up to – Europe. The world that you see is from the place that is projected as *"Paradise"*, the most cultured and civilized place on earth and the most desirous place as far as most Africans are concerned. This is the place where most of our people want to go to. But you, who were born and raised in this place, Europe, know it better than any of us in America or on the African continent. We must listen to your words because your view comes from the *"horse's own mouth"*! I thank you.

Mama Kali

Our Day Has Come:
To Warrior Sistas-True Pan African Women

Dear Sistas,

We don't get much news here in Ghana. I have given my TV away to the children at the Grandmother's House in Cape Coast (*Grandmothers in Ghana* now have a residence). My Ghanaian elder friend, told me more than a year ago that Obama would be president of America. I told him that, "***No way would white people allow this.***"

I now realize that white people always look to African people to save them, either in America or Europe, when they dig themselves into a ravine they expect black people to rescue them. We always do. It is obvious that white people don't know how to stop themselves from their own destructive actions. Is this where we are today, on this mad dash to destruction and total annihilation of our planet earth? There is *no one to turn to expect God's chosen people, the Africans and Aboriginals,* who can bring us out of this abyss.

As our great historian, Dr. John Henrick Clarke used to tell us, "*It is their nature, (Europeans); you can't keep a dog from barking; you can't keep the white people from fighting*". It would be helpful to read the ***Ice Man Inheritance***, and ***The Chosen People of the Caucuses***. The author has done a good job describing the nature of the Europeans without prejudice. The author is European Jew.

The Ghanaian Elder believes that Obama is guided by a much higher power and that a spiritual intervention is at work. I received an email last Nov-Dec about Obama being a "*Walk-In*". I don't know if you remember receiving this email from me. Many people believed that I meant that he was a "*Shoe-In*", which means that he is certain to win.

A "*Walk-In*" is entirely different. A "*Walk-In*" is a very high spiritual being who inhabits the body of a human being at a time in history when the world must move forward to another level. Such a time is now. Our planet is in a state of *"flux"* with a polar shift that is imminent. We are at the end of a *"Great Age"* and the return of Our Great Mother, **Mother Elminia**. (see *Biblical Manna-The Spiritual Message for the New Millennium*). The polar shift foretells the rise of *Cepheus,* the *Ethiopian King,* as the new pole star after the great polar shift. This is the great *"shaking"* that is predicted by the *Aboriginal American Prophecies*. Science also confirms the inevitable polar shift. The earth is already wobbling.

The coming of *Cepheus, the Ethiopian King, predicts the rise of the* Black Race of people to take their rightful place on earth. Obama is the first phase; he is close enough to the earthlings and close enough to the Africans to make that preliminary step in the right direction. We thank Michelle Obama for her guidance and her *"bringing him up"*.

We should not worry about the mad dash to destruction that we see coming from the war-mongers, the Euro-Americans and Europeans. They are only playing their part in the grand picture.

We must play our part; we must raise our own vibration so that when the shift comes we will rise up with the ethers so that when all the dust settles, we can carry forth with a new and greater civilization. I have recommended the **Teachings of the North Scale Institute 7.10.42** as a starting place. You can download this **Guide to Teachings** and the **Teachings-7.10.42 at:**

www.northinstitute.com

For those of you who are really ready to hear who we are and where we come from, read *Blacks: The Race from Beyond the Stars* by Paul D. Duncan. This book is hard to find, and can be ordered from: Society of Illumination; P. O. Box 13338; Detroit, MI 48214. The cost when I bought the book several years ago was $16.95 + shipping & handling. It is printed by Harlo Press; 50

Victor; Detroit, MI, 48203.

I hope that I did not get too esoteric on you; I know that sometimes when I reach beyond this earthly plane, I loose some of our people. Those of us who are ready will hear; others will go their chosen way. Friends are always sending me encouragement; I received this one yesterday.

"We are the miracles that God made
To taste the bitter fruit of time
We are precious
And one day our suffering
Will turn into the wonders of the earth"

Let us taste this bitter fruit of Time with gladness, as we know that our day has come!

Amen
Mama Kali

Is it Menopause or is it Kundalini?

I have been having hot flashes since 1991 at least this is what my children said. I was in denial for several years, because I thought that I was too young, 46 years old, and I had never had any female problems, not even monthly cramps. I just couldn't figure out why at the end of my reproductive years, all the challenging symptoms related to a woman's health would descend upon me. After all, I had kept up a very good diet throughout the years, being mostly a vegetarian, with a good deal of my proteins from soy products (before the GMO's), especially tofu, which was supposed to contain natural hormones to help balance out the estrogen-progesterone imbalance associated with menopausal hotflashes.

Now, sixteen years later, I'm still experiencing the welling up of heat in my body. Of course, the severity of the hot flashes has subsided tremendously. I remember when, at the height of my *"flashes"* every 20 minutes, like clock work, the heat would well up, rising up through my body from the middle burner (solar plexus navel area), rising slowly through my central spine, until it reached the top of my head. At that time I would break out into a full sweat, like I was picking cotton in the hot sun on a Mississippi plantation. I tried every natural product on the market. In desperation I even tried the most widely prescribed drug for menopausal symptoms, *"Premarin"*. The doctor said that it would take at least three months of use before I could see any change, so I used it for four months. The sweating abated somewhat, but the *"flashes"* continued. They just wouldn't go away. So I decided to let Mother Nature take Her course, no matter what conditions I had to endure. I simply continued to eat well, exercise and wait, and wait and wait.

Now at the age of sixty-two, fast approaching sixty-three, I still feel the welling up of heat, culminating at the top of my head and causing a slight flushing in my face, with very little sweating. At night, I usually throw the sheet or covering off my body, to cool

243

down for a few minutes.

I have come to a point in my life where I realize that my early years of seeking Divine guidance and a Spiritual life, is still a coveted goal and aspiration. The many years of working and taking care of a family, cooking and cleaning and running a business, were good preparations, a training ground for understanding humanity's evolution, and how I fit into the Divine Plan. The past 18 months that I have spent in Ghana, mostly alone, with the wind and the ocean and the swaying coconut palms as my most constant companions, have given me the chance to calm myself, to unravel after the many years of stress associated with living in America while *Aboriginal*, a mother, a wife and a business owner. That is a bunch of stress!

I have begun to wonder if it is in the Divine Plan for a woman, after reaching the *"age of freedom"* to devote her life to spiritual development, to assist our *Divine Mother* in the Evolution of this Planet. When a mature woman finds herself in prayer and meditation, is this the time that the spiral, the energy of creation, the caduceus, the healing power of the Planet, looks for the *Mother Goddess'* helpers to move humanity forward? Have we women in this busy material world lost our way? Have we forgotten the role that we should be playing at the third quarter of our lives? Is that the reason why we have mistaken the *rising up of the Spiritual Energy,* the *Kundalini*, as a negative symptom of maturity, aging, rather than to understand the authority vested in us to channel and direct that power into a positive force in the assistance of the *Creative Genius of the Universe*, our **Divine Mother**?

I call upon the women in my age group, who are finally finding time for themselves and time for *"Spiritualizing"* their lives, to look at the body heat that continues to seek its source culminating in that seventh chakra, the thousand-petal lotus at the top of your head. *By realizing the Divine Purpose of your Life, you*

can engage this energy to transmute your life and direct it to the
ultimate goal of Spiritual Attainment.

Longing for the Matriarchy

"It's too hot in here!" I shouted, as I entered the sun-drenched room of the beachfront cottage. *"How can you stay in here with all this heat?? Turn on the fan!!"* I continued to shout at my business partner as I entered the room to give him a message.

"I like being in the womb," he said coolly. It was then that I knew that I had the answer.

What ails our African men is the longing for the peace, warmth, harmony, comfort and safety of the Mother's womb. African societies from the very beginning have been Matriarchy Societies. What else could they be? After all, it is the woman who came first, who introduced the Virgin Birth from her own Essence, who brought forth humanity from the very cradle of the earth, our Mother of all life forms.

How could any society thrive if it is not led by the Mother? Who will know best how to lead, how to nurture, how to teach, how to defend except the one, who at the inception of human societies, was the progenitor of all institutions?

It is for this reason, the elimination of the Mother principle that the Earth on this very day -- is in flames! When the male energy assumes leadership we loose track of that element which governs in the interest of the society as a whole. Over the past Age lasting approximately 2160 years the world has been governed by the Patriarchal male energy of the Judea-Christian-Islamic world. Since the beginning of the 2,160 year era the world has been at war – constantly. The wars have been small, local conflict; they have been waged as larger national disputes called *"civil wars."* The wars have been global and called *"world wars."* But the wars have been constant.

Those who have ruled on this planet during this time of unending conflict have been men who had big problems with their female counterpart. It was not until the dawning of the **Age of**

Aries, about 4,400 years ago, that the **Mother Principle** was sidelined, given a *back seat,* sent to *the back of the bus!* With the rise of Judaism the Patriarchy gradually introduced the male energy and replaced the **Great Mother**. When the Age of Pisces rose, accompanied by the Christian religion, the **Great Mother** was totally displaced by the *"Holy Spirit."* **The woman was completely removed from the Trinity;** that is, the *Father, Son and Holy Spirit instead of the Mother, the Father and the Son.* The lie was told that She, the Great Mother, came from the rib of a man, that She committed the ultimate sin which caused mankind to be removed from the Garden of Eden, and for that reason, the woman would be forever cursed!

At this juncture in time humanity took on a non-human cloak; it bore a sword rather than a shaft of wheat and a shield rather than the scale of justice. *When the Christian religion was usurped from the Ethiopian Coptic Church by the* **Roman Emperor Constantine** *at the* **Council of Nicaea in 324 AD,** *Christianity became a religion plagued by war, sorrow, misery and genocide.* This is the fate of humanity under the Patriarchy, the male dominated society.

Now that we have passed through the **Age of Pisces** and entering into the **Age of Aquarius,** the time has come for humanity to *take on the characteristics of Divine Beings* and *rise to the height of Spirituality that the Soul can realize.* **It is only the Divine Mother who will allow Her children to rise to meet Her.** This is Her Dream, Her Desire, for those whom She nurtured within Her womb, knowing that when those children understand who they are, and who She is, we would know Peace, Harmony, Prosperity and live in a Paradise, in the Garden of Eden, on this planet Earth.

Thank you for your understanding;
Mama Kali Sichen
Amen Uati

Worth of a Woman

One Flaw In Women

Women have strengths that amaze men.
They bear hardships and they carry burdens,
but they hold happiness, love and joy.
They smile when they want to scream.
They sing when they want to cry.
They cry when they are happy
and laugh when they are nervous.
They fight for what they believe in.
They stand up to injustice.
They don't take "no" for an answer
when they believe there is a better solution.
They go without so their family can have.
They go to the doctor with a frightened friend.
They love unconditionally.
They cry when their children excel
and cheer when their friends get awards.
They are happy when they hear about
a birth or a wedding.
Their hearts break when a friend dies.

They grieve at the loss of a family member,
yet they are strong when they
think there is no strength left.
They know that a hug and a kiss
can heal a broken heart.
Women come in all shapes, sizes and colors.
They'll drive, fly, walk, run or e-mail you
to show how much they care about you.

The heart of a woman is what makes the world keep turning.
They bring joy, hope and love.
They have the compassion and ideas.
They give moral support to their family and friends.
Women have vital things to say and everything to give.
HOWEVER, IF THERE IS ONE FLAW IN WOMEN, IT IS THAT THEY FORGET THEIR WORTH
Author Unknown
Please pass this along to all your women friends and relatives to remind them just how amazing they are

Change is Good!

The only thing in the entire universe that is absolutely certain is **Change**. *Change* is the true condition of reality. Therefore, resistance to Change is not only a frustrating activity, it is fruitless exercise. The assured cycles of Mother Nature are our best indicators of the certainty of Change. Without any prompting from the human element on Earth, our Mother goes about Her motions of creating and destroying, while She constantly provides us with surprises of Her magnificent wonders.

The quote that people so often use, *"The devil you know is better than the angel you don't know"* had to come from the mouth of the devil himself. Such a philosophy shows that you resist Change and you fear what is just around the corner, so you stay where you are. This is an unnatural act because whether you make a move or not everything around you will Change.

For this reason the wise among us say that *"It is better to make the wrong move than to make no move at all"*. Surely in making that *"wrong"* move you have created your own destiny. But if you *"wait for something to happen"* you are at the mercy of those unknown architects, they who originated the reality that you find yourself in when you feared to make the next move.

Resistance to Change is a selfish act. When we close the door to Change we cut off the next phase of our own good. Sure, there are cycles within cycles, and sometimes there is an unwanted or uncomfortable Change that we don't want to experience. Live through it we must, because without that encounter we may not recognize the next opportunity that comes knocking at our door. We could very well *"miss the boat"* that we waited our entire lives to board.

Our great African leader **Osagyefo Dr. Kwame Nkrumah** reminded all of us that *"When you educate a man, you educate an individual; when you educate a woman you educate a nation."*

250

This wisdom is at the root of *"self-less-ness"* which is the condition of **MOST** women. Without even trying women give all that they have to the children that they carry for nine months in their wombs. Even after their birth most women will give all for their children and certainly whatever she knows she will impart to her children.

Women understand Change because our Great Mother included women in Her lunar cycles, the cycles that connect us to the ebb and flow of the universal spirit of water. By giving women the dominion over the Life-Death-Life cycles of the human species She entrusted us to assure the steady progression of humanity on Earth. The oldest female species, the Aboriginal woman, is truly the master of our future. Science has shown the Aboriginal women are the Mother of all humans; her dominion can not be denied.

The time has come for the world to move aside and allow the African and American Aboriginal woman (**including all of her** *"Aborigine"* sisters world-wide), to show the way. Her presence is warranted everywhere, needed in the White Houses of the world, the Black Houses and Your House. *By allowing our Great Mother Nature to implement the cycles of Change unimpeded, we allow our Future to Shine Bright!*

(Popular Song of the 1970's sung by George Benson)

Everything must Change
Nothing stays the same
Everything must Change
Nothing and no one stays the same
The Young become the Old
And Mysteries do unfold
But that's the way of Time
Nothing and no one goes unchanged
There are not many things in Life you can be sure of—
Except:

Rain falls from the clouds,
Sun lights up the sky
And hummingbirds do fly!

Freedom from Oppression Equals
Abnormal Behavior

The Falsification of Afrikan Consciousness by Amos Wilson should be required reading for any Aboriginal American who calls himself *"educated"*. In fact, this book should be required reading for any Aboriginal or African in high school or junior secondary school on the continent or in any nations where the Aborigines resides. Why? Because it so clearly outlines the psychosis of oppression of the Aboriginal mind and Aboriginal culture, Aboriginal history, why we fail to see the sources of our problems and why we feel so helpless to change our situation.

This book, published almost 25 years ago, is one of the gems of the struggle for the **Aboriginal global liberation**. In fact, it is said by many that Dr. Amos Wilson is no longer with us because he told the truth so clearly, without mincing his words, that he made the **Establishment** very uncomfortable. If Amos Wilson's work received the exposure that Bill Cosby received on his denouncement of **Aboriginal Americans** for our faults and our *alleged* shortcomings, there would be a revolution under way in America that would be irreversible.

Of course, Bill Cosby's statements served the purpose of the **White Supremacy Establishment,** i.e., to reestablish the Aboriginal inferiority and to reiterate our own responsibility for those shortcomings, while at the same time, not blaming the political and social structure and societal responsibility for our predicament. *Blaming the victim* totally for his own condition supports the ongoing suppression and subjugation of the Aboriginal American consciousness and aids and abets the continuation of the *White Apartheid Regime* in *America*.

To take Amos Wilson's book as a course study for a full semester would cause a reversal of thinking in any young mind that is open and ready for change, any kind of change. One does not have to be a radical or a revolutionary to see clearly how the dissection and analysis of the Aboriginal predicament, as outlined by Dr. Wilson, clears up some of the cob webs that cloud the Aboriginal mind from perceiving its true predicament.

This is not an easy book to read. In fact, I just finished reading it for the second time, and I know that if I read the book a third time, I will really grasp the deepest concepts that Dr. Wilson outlined so vividly. Hence, I believe that if the right teacher takes the time to dissect and dialog with the students, chapter by chapter, the student would emerge as a more competent, informed, stronger, more *conscious champion for the liberation of the Aboriginal mind and the end of White Supremacy global domination.*

Search the used book stores and the internet for *The Falsification of Afrikan Consciousness* by Amos Wilson. Buy one for a friend, forgo the next lunch date and plan book parties around the study of this treatise. You will emerge the winner!

An outlined version of *The Falsification of Afrikan Consciousness* is on the **North Scale Institute's** web site.

www.northscaleinstitute.com

Epilogue

As I look back over the past 17 years since I first ran away to Ghana, I weep because of the conditions that my people are immersed within. Many of our families have passed into the realm of the ancestors; so many of the Elders are no longer here to guide us. We who gathered in Ghana for Grandmothers' *"think tank"* are now the *"Elders"* in charge of passing on the familial truths that have guided and protected our people for eternity. Not only have our Elders passed away, but so have too many of our grand-children, our nieces and nephews, our relatives who did not reach the age of maturity. Most did not leave *"heirs"* to carry on their legacy. There is a gap in our linage – a hole in the eternal Soul of our people. There is an absence of numerous child-baring descendants.

We must face certain *"facts."* For the past 500 years, the Indigenous people of the world have been under a brutal attack. It's called GENOCIDE. We talk about it in hushed voices, as if we are afraid that we, ourselves, are committing a crime. Our *"crime"* is that we are **NOT** fighting back. Too many of us are waiting for some *"Savior"* to come to our rescue. **WE are the *"Saviors!"*** Too many years have transpired since the Grandmothers took a stand. We did not stand strong enough, speak long enough, organize widely enough to affect that change that we must realize. We MUST do better; otherwise, there will be no descendants left to fight for the survival of our species.

In this changing world, this GLOBAL TRANSFORMATION, we have the help of the Cosmos to bring about the changes that we must adopt.
The TIME to set into motion those metaphysical helpers – the angels, the cherubim, the seraphim, the knowing of the cosmic forces (Sun, Moon, Planets). All these guardians are at work on

our behalf right now. We must let go of our FEAR and move forward.

This is our time to return to the land of our Ancestors, where our people lie is graves, waiting for us to WAKE UP. For American Indians, the copper-colored Indigenous people of the Americas, we must return to OUR ancestral land to liberate ourselves FIRST! How can we devote our lives to the liberation of someone else's land when our children are dying by the millions in the land that our Fathers fought for died for hundreds of years?

Our lack of Unity is the result of our disunity in defining who we really are! *Too many of us define ourselves by a religious belief, i.e., Muslims, Christians, and all its denominations, Hebrew Israelites (Jews), even Buddhists and Hindus*. All of these are **Beliefs/Tags**! None of these "*tags*" define who you are – your lineage, your bloodline. "**American Indian**" is even another "*tag*"! We never called ourselves "*Indians*." In this publication, I used the tag "*Indian*" so that there would be no question as to who this treatise is about.

The Nobel Drew Ali taught us that we "*Moors*," are descendant from the ancient tribes of Moabites, Canaanites, i.e., descendants of Ham, the *Hamites*. Others describe the Aboriginal people of the Americas as descendants of Shem, or *Shemites*. When Abram, aka Abraham, was told to lead his people to a new land, this new land was America. The world "**Hebrew**" means "*those who crossed over*." Much controversy has ensued worldwide in the last year regarding the *Hebrews*, i.e., who are the **Real Hebrews?**
Dr. Ivan van Sertima, a noted Guyanese author and history professor wrote about the voyage of Masa Musa, Abu Bakr II, King of the rich and powerful Mali Empire, who sailed to America with 2,000 ships around 1311 AD. It is said that they found Moorish traders already in Brazil when their ships arrived. Hence, it does appear that the Muslim seafarers, the Moors, with recognized international trade routes, were well established in the

Americas. It is believed that the Olmecs were an earlier and acknowledged civilization long before that time. For how long? There is only conjecture. But surely, **the original copper-colored races were in the Americas long before Mansa Musa's voyage.**

The American Indians were described by many of the first explorers 300 years ago as having *"customs, religious ceremonies, and beliefs like the ancient Israelite, the Jews."* Many chroniclers of these *early explorers and settlers were Moors and Jews* from Europe, all melanated people running away from the **Spanish Inquisition**. They themselves were looking for a new home. They amalgamated with the Indigenous peoples all over the Americas. We can safely say that, at this time, more than 500 years of amalgamation, that **we are truly the Children of the Most High Creator – Fashioner of the Universe –** *The Great Mother/Father god.* **Nun and Nunet** – the great abyss, the hidden power, the dark void of the Universe, **the source of ALL. We are the SOURCE itself. We cannot be destroyed!**